THE ANNOTATED LUTHER STUDY EDITION

To the Christian Nobility of the German Nation

1520

THE ANNOTATED LUTHER STUDY EDITION

To the Christian Nobility of the German Nation

1520

JAMES M. ESTES

Timothy J. Wengert
EDITOR

Fortress Press
Minneapolis

To the Christian Nobility of the German Nation
Concerning the Improvement of the Christian Estate, 1520
THE ANNOTATED LUTHER STUDY EDITION

Unless otherwise noted, Scripture quotations are from New Revised Standard Version Bible, copyright © 1989 by the Division of Education of the National Council of Churches of Christ in the United States of America.

Excerpted from The Annotated Luther, Volume 1, *The Roots of Reform* (Minneapolis: Fortress Press, 2015), Timothy J. Wengert, volume editor.

Fortress Press Publication Staff:
Scott Tunseth, Project Editor
Marissa Wold Uhrina, Production Manager
Laurie Ingram, Cover Design
Esther Diley, Permissions

Copyeditor: David Lott
Series design and typesetting: Ann Delgehausen, Trio Bookworks
Proofreader: Laura Weller

Library of Congress Cataloging-in-Publication Data is available

Print ISBN: 978-1-5064-1349-5
eISBN: 978-1-5064-1350-1

The paper used in this publication meets the minimum requirements of American National Standard for Information Sciences—Permanence of Paper for Printed Library Materials, ANSI Z329, 48-1984.

Manufactured in the U.S.A.

Contents

Publisher's Note

About the Annotated Luther Study Edition

The volumes in the Annotated Luther Study Edition series have first been published in one of the comprehensive volumes of The Annotated Luther series. A description of that series and the volumes can be found in the Series Introduction (p. vii). While each comprehensive Annotated Luther volume can easily be used in classroom settings, we also recognize that treatises are often assigned individually for reading and study. To facilitate classroom and group use, we have pulled key treatises along with their introductions, annotations, and images directly from the Annotated Luther Series volumes.

Please note that the study edition page numbers match the page numbers of the larger Annotated Luther volume in which it first appeared. We have intentionally retained the same page numbering to facilitate use of the study editions and larger volumes side by side.

To the Christian Nobility of the German Nation, 1520,
was first published in The Annotated Luther series,
Volume 1, *The Roots of Reform* (2015).

Series Introduction

Engaging the Essential Luther

Even after five hundred years Martin Luther continues to engage and challenge each new generation of scholars and believers alike. With 2017 marking the five-hundredth anniversary of Luther's *95 Theses*, Luther's theology and legacy are being explored around the world with new questions and methods and by diverse voices. His thought invites ongoing examination, his writings are a staple in classrooms and pulpits, and he speaks to an expanding assortment of conversation partners who use different languages and hale from different geographical and social contexts.

The six volumes of The Annotated Luther edition offer a flexible tool for the global reader of Luther, making many of his most important writings available in the *lingua franca* of our times as one way of facilitating interest in the Wittenberg reformer. They feature new introductions, annotations, revised translations, and textual notes, as well as visual enhancements (illustrations, art, photos, maps, and timelines). The Annotated Luther edition embodies Luther's own cherished principles of communication. Theological writing, like preaching, needs to reflect human beings' lived experience, benefits from up-to-date scholarship, and should be easily accessible to all. These volumes are designed to help teachers and students, pastors and laypersons, and other professionals in ministry understand the context in which the documents were written, recognize how the documents have shaped Protestant and Lutheran thinking, and interpret the meaning of these documents for faith and life today.

The Rationale for This Edition

For any reader of Luther, the sheer number of his works presents a challenge. Well over one hundred volumes comprise the scholarly edition of Luther's works, the so-called Weimar Ausgabe (WA), a publishing enterprise begun in 1883 and only completed in the twenty-first century. From 1955 to 1986, fifty-five volumes came to make up *Luther's Works* (American Edition) (LW), to which Concordia Publishing House, St. Louis, is adding still more. This English-language contribution to Luther studies, matched by similar translation projects for Erasmus of Rotterdam and John Calvin, provides a theological and historical gold mine for those interested in studying Luther's thought. But even these volumes are not always easy to use and are hardly portable. Electronic forms have increased availability, but preserving Luther in book form and providing readers with manageable selections are also important goals.

Moreover, since the publication of the WA and the first fifty-five volumes of the LW, research on the Reformation in general and on Martin Luther in particular has broken new ground and evolved, as has knowledge regarding the languages in which Luther wrote. Up-to-date information from a variety of sources is brought together in The Annotated Luther, building on the work done by previous generations of scholars. The language and phrasing of the translations have also been updated to reflect modern English usage. While the WA and, in a derivative way, LW remain the central source for Luther scholarship, the present critical and annotated English translation facilitates research internationally and invites a new generation of readers for whom Latin and German might prove an unsurpassable obstacle to accessing Luther. The WA provides the basic Luther texts (with some exceptions); the LW provides the basis for almost all translations.

Defining the "Essential Luther"

Deciding which works to include in this collection was not easy. Criteria included giving attention to Luther's initial key works; considering which publications had the most impact in his day and later; and taking account of Luther's own favorites, texts addressing specific issues of continued importance for today, and Luther's exegetical works. Taken as a whole, these works present the many sides of Luther, as reformer, pastor, biblical interpreter, and theologian. To serve today's readers and by using categories similar to those found in volumes 31–47 of Luther's works (published by Fortress Press), the volumes offer in the main a thematic rather than strictly chronological approach to Luther's writings. The volumes in the series include:

> Volume 1: *The Roots of Reform* (Timothy J. Wengert, editor)
> Volume 2: *Word and Faith* (Kirsi I. Stjerna, editor)
> Volume 3: *Church and Sacraments* (Paul W. Robinson, editor)
> Volume 4: *Pastoral Writings* (Mary Jane Haemig, editor)
> Volume 5: *Christian Life in the World* (Hans J. Hillerbrand, editor)
> Volume 6: *The Interpretation of Scripture* (Euan K. Cameron, editor)

The History of the Project

In 2011 Fortress Press convened an advisory board to explore the promise and parameters of a new English edition of Luther's essential works. Board members Denis Janz, Robert Kolb, Peter Matheson, Christine Helmer, and Kirsi Stjerna deliberated with

Fortress Press publisher Will Bergkamp to develop a concept and identify contributors. After a review with scholars in the field, college and seminary professors, and pastors, it was concluded that a single-language edition was more desirable than dual-language volumes.

In August 2012, Hans Hillerbrand, Kirsi Stjerna, and Timothy Wengert were appointed as general editors of the series with Scott Tunseth from Fortress Press as the project editor. The general editors were tasked with determining the contents of the volumes and developing the working principles of the series. They also helped with the identification and recruitment of additional volume editors, who in turn worked with the general editors to identify volume contributors. Mastery of the languages and unique knowledge of the subject matter were key factors in identifying contributors. Most contributors are North American scholars and native English speakers, but The Annotated Luther includes among its contributors a circle of international scholars. Likewise, the series is offered for a global network of teachers and students in seminary, university, and college classes, as well as pastors, lay teachers, and adult students in congregations seeking background and depth in Lutheran theology, biblical interpretation, and Reformation history.

Editorial Principles

The volume editors and contributors have, with few exceptions, used the translations of LW as the basis of their work, retranslating from the WA for the sake of clarity and contemporary usage. Where the LW translations have been substantively altered, explanatory notes have often been provided. More importantly, contributors have provided marginal notes to help readers understand theological and historical references. Introductions have been expanded and sharpened to reflect the very latest historical and theological research. In citing the Bible, care has been taken to reflect the German and Latin texts commonly used in the sixteenth century rather than modern editions, which often employ textual sources that were unavailable to Luther and his contemporaries.

Finally, all pieces in The Annotated Luther have been revised in the light of modern principles of inclusive language. This is not always an easy task with a historical author, but an intentional effort has been made to revise language throughout, with creativity and editorial liberties, to allow Luther's theology to speak free from unnecessary and unintended gender-exclusive language. This important principle provides an opportunity to translate accurately certain gender-neutral German and Latin expressions that Luther employed—for example, the Latin word *homo* and the German *Mensch* mean "human being," not simply "males." Using the words *man* and *men* to translate such terms would create an ambiguity not present in the original texts. The focus is on linguistic accuracy and Luther's intent. Regarding creedal formulations and trinitarian language, Luther's own expressions have been preserved, without entering the complex and important contemporary debates over language for God and the Trinity.

The 2017 anniversary of the publication of the *95 Theses* is providing an opportunity to assess the substance of Luther's role and influence in the Protestant Reformation. Revisiting Luther's essential writings not only allows reassessment of Luther's rationale and goals but also provides a new look at what Martin Luther was about and why new generations would still wish to engage him. We hope these six volumes offer a compelling invitation.

Hans J. Hillerbrand
Kirsi I. Stjerna
Timothy J. Wengert
General Editors

Abbreviations

BC	*The Book of Concord*, ed. Robert Kolb and Timothy J. Wengert (Minneapolis: Fortress Press, 2000).
Brecht 1	Martin Brecht, *Martin Luther: His Road to Reformation, 1483–1521*, trans. James L. Schaaf (Minneapolis: Fortress Press, 1985).
CA	*Augsburg Confession*
CR	*Corpus Reformatorum: Philippi Melanthonis opera quae supersunt omnia*, ed. Karl Brettschneider and Heinrich Bindseil, 28 vols. (Braunschweig: Schwetchke, 1834–1860).
DWB	*Deutsches Wörterbuch*, ed. Jakob and Wilhelm Grimm, 16 vols. in 32 parts (Leipzig, 1854–1960).
Friedberg	*Corpus iuris canonici*, ed. Emil Friedberg, 2 vols. (Leipzig: Tauchnitz, 1879–1881).
LC	*Large Catechism*
LW	*Luther's Works* (American edition), ed. Helmut Lehmann and Jaroslav Pelikan, 55 vols. (Philadelphia: Fortress Press/St. Louis: Concordia Publishing House, 1955–1986).
MLStA	*Martin Luther: Studienausgabe*, ed. Hans-Ulrich Delius, 6 vols. (Berlin/Leipzig: Evangelische Verlagsanstalt, 1979–1999).
MPL	*Patrologiae cursus completus, series Latina*, ed. Jacques-Paul Migne, 217 vols. (Paris, 1815–1875).
NPNF	*Nicene and Post-Nicene Fathers*, ed. Philip Schaaf and Henry Wace, series 1, 14 vols.; series 2, 14 vols. (London/New York: T&T Clark, 1886–1900).
RTA	Adolf Wrede et al., eds., *Deutsche Reichtagsakten, jüngere Reihe*, 20 vols. (Gotha: Perthes, 1893–2009).
WA	*Luthers Werke: Kritische Gesamtausgabe [Schriften]*, 73 vols. (Weimar: H. Böhlau, 1883–2009).
WA Br	*Luthers Werke: Kritische Gesamtausgabe: Briefwechsel*, 18 vols. (Weimar: H. Böhlau, 1930–1985).
WA DB	*Luthers Werke: Kritische Gesamtausgabe: Deutsche Bibel*, 12 vols. (Weimar: H. Böhlau, 1906–1961).
WA TR	*Luthers Werke: Kritische Gesamtausgabe: Tischreden*, 6 vols. (Weimar: H. Böhlau, 1912–1921).
Wander	Karl F. W. Wander, ed., *Deutsches Sprichwörterlexikon: Ein Hausschatz für das deutsche Volk*, 5 vols. (Leipzig: Brockhaus, 1867–1880; reprint Aalen: Scientia, 1963).

To the Christian Nobility of the German Nation Concerning the

Improvement of the Christian Estate

1520

JAMES M. ESTES

INTRODUCTION

This treatise is Luther's first appeal to secular authorities for help with the reform of the church. For more than two years, starting with the *95 Theses* in 1517, Luther's appeals for reform had been addressed to the ecclesiastical hierarchy, whose divinely imposed responsibility for such things he took for granted. By the early months of 1520, however, Luther had come to the conclusion that nothing could be expected from Rome but intransigent opposition to reform of any sort.[a] It was only at this point that he began to write of the need for secular rulers to intervene with measures that would clear the way for ecclesiastical reform. In the *Treatise on Good Works* (in print by 8 June 1520), Luther argued that the abuses of "the spiritual authorities" were causing "Christendom to go to ruin," and that, in this emergency, anyone who was able to do so should help in whatever way possible. Specifically, "The best and indeed the only remaining remedy would be for kings, princes, the nobility, cities, and communities

---

a   See James M. Estes, *Peace, Order, and the Glory of God: Secular Authority and the Church in the Thought of Luther and Melanchthon, 1518–1559* (Leiden: Brill, 2005), 7–17. See also Brecht 1:369–79.

to take the first step in the matter so that the bishops and clergy, who are now fearful, would have cause to follow."[b] He made the same point in the treatise *On the Papacy in Rome* (in print by 26 June 1520), asserting that "the horrible disgrace of Christendom" has gone so far "that there is no more hope on earth except with secular authority."[c]

Meanwhile, just as the *Treatise on Good Works* was coming off the presses, Luther received a copy of the *Epitome of a Response to Martin Luther* (*Epitoma responsionis ad Martinum Lutherum*) by the papal theologian Silvester Prierias (c. 1426-1523).[1] The *Epitome* was a bold assertion of papal absolutism, insisting that papal authority was superior to that of a council and even to Scripture itself. To Luther, this "hellish book" was conclusive evidence that the Antichrist was reigning in Rome and that there was no possibility of a reform initiated or approved by it. It was therefore necessary to abandon "unhappy, hopeless, blasphemous Rome" and seek reform elsewhere.[d]

It was in this frame of mind that on 7 June 1520 Luther announced to Georg Spalatin (1484-1545) his intention "to issue a broadside to [Emperor] Charles and the nobility of Germany against the tyranny and baseness of the Roman Curia."[e] By 23 June, the "broadside" had grown into a major treatise, the manuscript of which Luther sent to his friend Nicholas von Amsdorf (1483-1565), together with the letter that became the preface to the treatise when it was published in mid-August.[f] In the letter, Luther describes the treatise as "a few points on the matter of the improvement of the state of Christendom, to be laid before the Christian nobility of the German nation, in the hope that God may help his church through the laity, since the clergy, to whom this task more properly belongs, have grown quite irresponsible."[2] What could the laity do to remedy the failure of the clergy?

1. The Dominican, Silvestro Mazzolini, known as Sylvester Prierias (after his birthplace Priero in Piedmont), was "master of the sacred palace" at the Roman Curia, which meant that he was the pope's theological adviser and censor of books. Given charge of the Luther case in 1518, he became Luther's first Italian literary opponent, publishing four polemical treatises against him in the years 1518–1520. The third of these, the *Epitome*, was published at Perugia in 1519.

2. See below, p. 376. Offers of support, including armed protection, received in the early months of 1520 from the imperial knights Ulrich von Hutten (1488–1523), Franz von Sickingen (1481–1523), and Silvester von Schaumberg (c. 1466–1534) appear to have given Luther a sense of political support outside Saxony that encouraged him to hope that an appeal to the nobility might well produce a positive response; see Brecht 1:369–70.

b   See above, p. 342.

c   LW 39:102–3.

d   WA 6:328–29 (Luther's preface to the annotated edition of the *Epitome* that he published in mid-June 1520).

e   WA Br 2:120.

f   See below, pp. 376–78.

Luther's answer was that the leaders of the lay community could summon a church council.[g] But how could that be done against the will of the pope? Luther's answer to that question was a fundamental contribution to the thought of the Reformation.

The treatise itself is divided into three sections. In the first, Luther attacks the "three walls" behind which the "Romanists" have shielded themselves from reform: (1) the claim that spiritual authority is higher than secular authority and therefore not subject to secular jurisdiction; (2) the claim that the pope alone has the authority to interpret the Scriptures; and (3) the claim that only the pope can summon a council. The second section is a brief discussion of measures to be discussed at councils to curb the "thievery, trickery, and tyranny" of Rome. The third and by far the longest of the three sections, which appears to have been tacked on at the last moment, is a set of twenty-seven proposals for action by either secular authority or a council (as appropriate) for improving "the dreadful state of affairs" in Christendom. In these last two sections, Luther denounces a long list of ecclesiastical abuses, particularly those of the Roman Curia, which would have been familiar to his readers. Many of them are taken directly from the lists of "*Gravamina* [grievances] of the German Nation Against Rome" that had been brought forward at virtually every meeting of the imperial diet since the middle of the fifteenth century, most recently at the Diet of Augsburg in 1518.[h] In so doing, Luther identified himself with the conciliarist, patriotically German, anti-Roman sentiment that pervaded German ecclesiastical and political life at the time. This was well calculated to secure widespread popular approval for the treatise, but

g   For Luther's suspicions about church councils, see p. 341 above.

h   See Martin Luther, *Sämmtliche Werke*, ed. Johann Georg Walch et al., 2d ed., vol. 15: *Reformations-Schriften, erste Abtheilung, zur Reformationshistorie gehörige Documente: A. Wider die Papisten aus den Jahren 1517 bis 1524.* (St. Louis: Concordia, 1899), 453–71. For the more extensive list presented at the Diet of Worms in 1521, see RTA 2:661–718.

it is Luther's attack on the three walls that accounts for the enduring importance of the treatise. In that attack he redefines the relationship between clergy and laity and elaborates the view of the role of secular government in church reform to which he would adhere virtually without change for the remainder of the 1520s, before adapting it to new circumstances in the 1530s.

To the Christian Nobility has often been described as the work in which Luther called upon the German princes to assume responsibility for the reform of the church.[i] In fact, however, the most striking feature of the treatise is Luther's refusal to attribute to secular rulers any authority at all in matters of faith or church governance. Although the classical formulation of what is sometimes labeled the "Doctrine of the Two Kingdoms" was still three years in the future,[j] Luther was already clearly committed to the view that secular authority extends only to the secular realm of human affairs and that it has no jurisdiction in the spiritual realm. As he put it in the *Treatise on Good Works*, secular jurisdiction is limited to matters covered by the Second Table of the Decalogue (the commandments regulating the conduct of human beings toward one another), and that it has nothing to do with the First Table (the commandments regulating the duties of human beings toward God).[k] How, then, could Luther justify any role at all for secular government in the reform of the church? The answer, already prefigured in the *Treatise on Good Works* and *The Papacy at Rome* and now fully elaborated in *To the Christian Nobility*, was necessarily somewhat complicated.

---

i   See, e.g., John Dillenberger's introduction to the treatise in *Martin Luther: Selections from His Writings* (New York: Random House, 1961), 403: "In this work of 1520 . . . Luther calls upon the ruling class to reform the Church, since the Church will not reform itself." See also Roland Bainton, *Here I Stand: A Life of Martin Luther* (New York/Nashville: Abingdon, 1950), 152: "[B]y what right, the modern reader might well inquire, might Luther call upon [the German nobility] to reform the Church?"

j   In the treatise *On Secular Authority, To What Extent It Should Be Obeyed* (LW 45:75–129).

k   See above, pp. 342–44.

First of all, many of the most glaring ecclesiastical abuses in need of correction fell into the category of secular crimes (robbery and theft) committed by "spiritual" persons (the clergy and monks). Thus defined, such abuses (e.g., raising money by peddling indulgences) could be viewed as the direct responsibility of secular rulers, to whom God had assigned the duty of protecting the goods and property of their subjects. One had only to dispose of the claimed exemption of "spiritual" persons from secular jurisdiction. "Spiritual" crimes, on the other hand, were a more difficult matter. Given his definition of the limits of secular authority, Luther could not appeal to secular rulers *as such* to deal with such matters. He could, however, argue that, *as baptized Christians*, secular rulers shared in the right and duty of all Christians to interpret Scripture and to adhere to the correct interpretation if the pope errs. This meant that in an emergency with which the pope could not or would not deal, they shared in the right and duty of all baptized Christians to do what they could to restore ecclesiastical authority to its proper function. It meant further that, *because of their commanding position in society*, they had a special obligation to do so. On this basis, Luther could appeal to the emperor and the German princes to serve their fellow Christians in an emergency by summoning a church council, in which "bishops and clergy," hitherto intimidated and frustrated by papal opposition to reform, would be free to do their duty to provide reform. The aim, in other words, was to restore the proper functioning of established ecclesiastical authority, not to transfer it to secular rulers.[1]

The response to Luther's appeal to "the Christian nobility of the German nation" came at the Diet of Worms in 1521. Instead of summoning a reform council, the assembled princes outlawed Luther and his followers. But the reform movement continued to spread rapidly, particularly in cities and towns, and Luther defended the right of such communities to reform themselves despite the objections of

---

[1]   See Estes, *Peace, Order, and the Glory of God,* 17–30.

Luther is shown as an Augustinian monk debating the pope,
a cardinal, a bishop, and another monk.

ecclesiastical authority.*ᵐ* When, moreover, hostile Catholic
governments tried to suppress these reform efforts, Luther
angrily denounced them for arrogating to themselves a
power in spiritual matters that was not theirs by right.*ⁿ* By
the late 1520s, however, the spontaneous spread of the Reformation in Saxony had reached the point at which church
life urgently needed to be regulated in the interest of unity
and good order. But Saxony had no bishop to provide the

m   See LW 39:305–14 (*That a Christian Assembly or Congregation Has the
    Right and Power to Judge All Teaching and to Call, Appoint, and Dismiss
    Teachers, Established and Proven by Scripture*, 1523).

n   *On Secular Authority* (1523).

necessary leadership. In this emergency, Luther once again appealed to secular authority for help with ecclesiastical reform, using essentially the same arguments that he had advanced in 1520. He called on the elector, in his capacity as Christian brother, to serve his fellow Christians by appointing an ecclesiastical visitation commission that would establish uniformity of doctrine and practice on the churches in his domains.[o] Since, however, Luther expected the elector *as prince* to enforce the established uniformity, it was clear that his distinction between the prince *as prince* (secular authority *as such*), without authority in spiritual matters, and the prince as Christian brother, entitled to intervene only in emergencies, no longer fit the situation as well as it had at the beginning of the decade. Luther himself was aware of this and, starting in 1530, he rethought his position in conversation with Philipp Melanchthon (1497-1560). By 1534 he and Melanchthon were in agreement that, the necessary distinction between secular and spiritual authority notwithstanding, it was the duty of a Christian prince to establish and maintain true religion among his subjects.[p]

o   LW 40:263-320.

p   See Estes, *Peace, Order, and the Glory of God*, ch. 5. In Luther's case,
    the key texts are his commentaries on Psalms 82 (1530) and 101
    (1534-35), particularly the latter; see LW 13:51-60, 166-201.

Portrait of Nicholaus von Amsdorf, whom Luther consecrated as bishop of Naumburg in the 1540s, by the German painter and printmaker Peter Gottlandt.

TO THE CHRISTIAN NOBILITY OF THE GERMAN NATION CONCERNING THE IMPROVEMENT OF THE CHRISTIAN ESTATE, 1520[3,4]

JESUS.[q]

TO THE ESTEEMED and Reverend Master, Nicholas von Amsdorf, Licentiate of Holy Scripture, and Canon of Wittenberg, my special and kind friend, from Doctor Martin Luther.

The grace and peace of God be with you, esteemed, reverend, and dear sir and friend.[r]

The time for silence is past, and the time to speak has come, as Eccles. [3:7] says. I am carrying out our intention to put together a few points on the matter of the improvement of the state of Christendom, to be laid before the Christian nobility of the German nation, in the hope that God may help his church through the laity, since the clergy, to whom this task more properly belongs, have grown quite irresponsible. I am sending the whole thing to you, reverend sir, [that you may give] an opinion on it and, where necessary, improve it.

I know full well that I shall not escape the charge of presumption, because I, a despised, cloistered person, venture to address such high and great estates on such weighty mat-

3. The present translation is a twice-revised version of that by Charles M. Jacobs in *Works of Martin Luther with Introductions and Notes*, ed. Luther Reed et al., 6 vols. (Philadelphia: Holman, 1915), 2:61–164. The first revision was by James Atkinson for LW 44:123–217. The German text used is that of MLStA 2:96–167, edited by Karlheinz Blaschke. Much information from Blaschke's notes has found its way into this translation. See also WA 6:381–469, and Karl Benrath, ed., *An den christlichen Adel deutscher Nation von des christlichen Standes Besserung* (Halle: Verein für Reformationsgeschichte, 1884), referred to below as Benrath.

q   See above, p. 264, n. 11.

r   An early example of Luther's use of a "Pauline greeting" (cf. 1 Cor. 1:3) here combined with an older form where he simply employed the word "Jesus." By 1522 this new form, an indication of identification of his office with that of the Apostle Paul, would completely replace the other.

ters, as if there were nobody else in the world except Doctor Luther to take up the cause of Christendom and give advice to such highly competent people. I make no apologies no matter who demands them. Perhaps I owe my God and the world another work of folly. I intend to pay my debt honestly. And if I succeed, I shall for the time being become a

A fool is pictured with a feather hat,
about to trip himself with a cane; one shoe on
and one off; and three children running about him.

court jester. And if I fail, I still have the one advantage that no one need buy me a cowl or provide me with a cockscomb.[5] It is a question of who will put the bells on whom.[s] I must fulfill the proverb, "Whatever the world does, a monk must be in the picture, even if he has to be painted in."[t] More than once a fool has spoken wisely, and wise men have often been arrant fools. Paul says, "He who wishes to be wise must

---

s   I.e., who will declare whom to be a clown.
t   The proverb *monachus semper praesens* is attested in Wander, 3:703, n. 130.

4. In the German phrase *der christliche Stand* ("the Christian Estate"), the word *stand* can mean "estate" as used in such phrases as "estates of the realm" or "imperial estates," but it can also mean "status" in the sense of standing or rank, as well as "state" in the sense of condition or walk of life. Nowhere in the treatise does Luther address himself to a Christian or "spiritual" estate that stands apart from another, presumably secular or worldly estate in society. Indeed, one of his principal arguments is that all baptized Christians are of the same "spiritual status" and that there is no distinction in this regard between clergy and laity (see below, pp. 381–83). Moreover, the list of reforms that he proposes requires action by both spiritual authority and secular authority, which he views as Christian. "The Christian estate," in other words, is the entire body of Christians viewed as one entity, often referred to as Christendom, in which all are of the same spiritual rank or standing. Luther finds that entity to be in terrible condition and thus sorely in need of reform. Bertram Lee Woolf captured this meaning when he took the liberty of turning *von des christlichen Standes Besserung* into "as to the Amelioration of the State of Christendom"; see Woolf, *Reformation Writings of Martin Luther* (New York: Philosophical Library, 1953), 101.

5. A cowl and a red rooster's comb were traditional signs of a clown or jester. Luther did not need them because he was already equipped with a monk's cowl and tonsure.

6. Luther's authority to speak on controversial matters of doctrine and practice derived from his status as a doctor of theology. In the process of being awarded his doctorate (19 October 1512), he took a solemn oath to teach the Holy Scriptures faithfully and to combat heresy and error. With the doctorate, moreover, he acquired full academic freedom to discuss without hindrance all questions of scriptural interpretation. See Brecht 1:126-27.

7. During the Great Schism in the Western church (1378-1417), when there were two (and, for a time, three) rival popes, and ecclesiastical abuses (most of them rooted in the ruthless exploitation of papal authority to raise money) got worse, a sustained attempt was made to deal with the situation by means of a general council. Canonists argued that supreme authority in the church rested not with the pope, but with the universal community of believers, and that in an emergency that authority could be exercised by a council, which could be convoked by some authority (e.g., the emperor) other than the pope. The resulting "conciliar movement" assigned to a general council the task of restoring the unity of Christendom under one pope and of reforming the church, beginning with a thorough reform of the papacy itself. The Council of Constance (1414-1417) managed to restore unity under one undisputed pope, but it did not successfully address the problem of church reform. There followed a struggle

become a fool" [1 Cor. 3:18]. Moreover, since I am not only a fool, but also a sworn doctor of Holy Scripture, I am glad for the opportunity to fulfill my doctor's oath,[6] even in the guise of a fool.

I beg you, give my apologies to those who are moderately intelligent, for I do not know how to earn the grace and favor of the super-intelligent. I have often sought to do so with the greatest pains, but from now on I neither desire nor value their favor. God help us to seek not our own glory but his alone. Amen.

At Wittenberg, in the monastery of the Augustinians, on the eve of St. John Baptist [June 23] in the year fifteen hundred and twenty.

To His Most Illustrious, Most Mighty, and Imperial Majesty, and to the Christian Nobility of the German Nation, from Doctor Martin Luther.

Grace and power from God, Most Illustrious Majesty, and most gracious and dear lords.

It is not from sheer impertinence or rashness that I, one poor man, have taken it upon myself to address your worships. All the estates of Christendom, particularly in Germany, are now oppressed by distress and affliction, and this has stirred not only me but everybody else to cry out time and time again and to pray for help. It has even compelled me now at this time to cry aloud that God may inspire someone with his Spirit to lend a helping hand to this distressed and wretched nation. Often the councils have made some pretense at reformation, but their attempts have been cleverly frustrated by the guile of certain men, and things have gone from bad to worse.[7] With God's help I intend to expose the wiles and wickedness of these men, so that they are shown up for what they are and may never again be so obstructive and destructive. God has given us a young man of noble birth as our ruler,[8] thus awakening great hope of good in many hearts. Presented with such an opportunity we ought to apply ourselves and use this time of grace profitably.

The first and most important thing to do in this matter is to prepare ourselves in all seriousness. We must not start something by trusting in great power or human reason, even if all the power in the world were ours. For God cannot and will not suffer that a good work begin by relying upon one's own power and reason. He dashes such works to the ground; they do no good at all. As it says in Ps. 33[:16], "No king is saved by his great might and no lord is saved by the greatness of his strength." I fear that this is why the good emperors Frederick (I) Barbarossa and Frederick II and many other German emperors, even though all the world feared them, were in former times shamefully oppressed and trodden underfoot by the popes.[9] It may be that they relied on their own might more than on God, and therefore had to fall.

Frederick I Barbarossa.

between the restored papacy, which rejected the very idea of conciliar supremacy and feared reforms that would reduce papal income, and the conciliarists, who were numerous among theologians, bishops, and secular rulers, and who continued to call for limitations on papal authority and a thorough reform of the church "in head and members." With the help of Europe's secular rulers, to whom they made far-reaching concessions of authority to appoint bishops and other clergymen as well as of a share of ecclesiastical revenues, the popes defeated the conciliar movement, which had its last stand at the Council of Basel (1431–1449). But because of abuse and lack of reform in the "Renaissance papacy," conciliarism retained widespread appeal, particularly north of the Alps.

8. Charles V (1500–1558) was now twenty years old.

9. The Hohenstaufen emperors Frederick (I) Barbarossa (1152–1190) and his grandson, Frederick II (1212–1250), the last of the Hohenstaufens, both pursued dynastic and imperial interests in Italy that brought them into conflict with the cities of Lombardy and the popes (in their capacity as Italian territorial rulers). Both were excommunicated, and Frederick II was even deposed; both experienced catastrophic losses on the battlefield at the hands of their Italian enemies. Meanwhile, particularly in the reign of Frederick II, the German princes secured concessions that put an end to all hope of the establishment of a powerful national monarchy hereditary in the Hohenstaufen family.

Imperial authority survived in northern Italy and Germany but real power was in the hands of the great commercial cities of Italy and the German territorial princes.

10. Known as "the warrior pope," Julius II (1443–1513) spent much of his reign (1503–13) personally leading military campaigns aimed at recovering papal territory that had been alienated by his predecessors or annexed by Venice. In these struggles, France and Venice numbered among his enemies, but the German emperor Maximilian I (1459–1519) was his occasional ally.

11. I.e., the advocates of papal supremacy in the church.

What was it in our own time that raised the bloodthirsty Julius II to such heights? Nothing else, I fear, except that France, the Germans, and Venice relied upon themselves.[10] The children of Benjamin slew forty-two thousand Israelites because the latter relied on their own strength, Judg. 20[:21].[u]

That it may not so fare with us and our noble Charles, we must realize that in this matter we are not dealing with human beings, but with the princes of hell. These princes might well fill the world with war and bloodshed, but war and bloodshed do not overcome them. We must tackle this job by renouncing trust in physical force and trusting humbly in God. We must seek God's help through earnest prayer and fix our minds on nothing else than the misery and distress of suffering Christendom without regard to what evil men deserve. Otherwise, we may start the game with great prospects of success, but when we get into it the evil spirits will stir up such confusion that the whole world will swim in blood, and then nothing will come of it all. Let us act wisely, therefore, and in the fear of God. The more force we use, the greater our disaster if we do not act humbly and in the fear of God. If the popes and Romanists[11] have hitherto been able to set kings against each other by the devil's help, they might well be able to do it again if we were to go ahead without the help of God on our own strength and by our own cunning.

The Romanists have very cleverly built three walls around themselves. Hitherto they have protected themselves by these walls in such a way that no one has been able to reform them. As a result, the whole of Christendom has fallen horribly.

In the first place, when secular authority has been used against them, they have made decrees and declared that secular authority has no jurisdiction over them, but that, on the contrary, spiritual authority is above secular authority.[v] In the second place, when the attempt is made to reprove

u   The biblical text mentions only twenty-two thousand slain.
v   See p. 384, n. 18.

them with the Scriptures, they raise the objection that only the pope may interpret the Scriptures.[w] In the third place, if threatened with a council, their story is that no one may summon a council but the pope.[x]

In this way they have cunningly stolen our three rods from us, so that they may go unpunished. They have ensconced themselves within the safe stronghold of these three walls so that they can practice all the knavery and wickedness that we see today. Even when they have been compelled to hold a council,[12] they have weakened its power in advance by putting the princes under oath to let them remain as they were.[y] In addition, they have given the pope full authority over all decisions of a council, so that it is all the same whether there are many councils or no councils. They only deceive us with puppet shows and sham fights. They fear terribly for their skin in a really free council! They have so intimidated kings and princes with this technique that they believe it would be an offense against God not to be obedient to the Romanists in all their knavish and ghoulish deceits.

May God help us and give us just one of those trumpets with which the walls of Jericho were knocked down [Josh. 6:20] to blow down these walls of straw and paper as well and set free the Christian rods for the punishment of sin,[13] [as well as] bring to light the craft and deceit of the devil, to the end that through punishment we may reform ourselves and once more attain God's favor.

Let us begin by attacking the first wall. It is pure invention that pope, bishop, priests, and monks are called the spiritual estate while princes, lords, artisans, and farmers are called the secular estate. This is indeed a piece of deceit and hypocrisy. Yet no one need be intimidated by it, and for this reason: all Christians are truly of spiritual status, and there is no difference among them except that of office. Paul says in 1 Cor. 12[:12-13] that we are all one body, yet every

12. The most recent was the Fifth Lateran Council, 1512–1517. See n. 40, p. 398.

13. "Rod" is used in the Bible to mean an instrument of God's wrath; see, e.g., Ps. 2:9 and Rev. 2:27.

w For the claim of sole authority to interpret Scripture, see Friedberg 1:58-60 (*Decret. prima pars*, dist. 19, can. 1f).

x See n. 37.

y See above, *Treatise on Good Works*, p. 341f.

member has its own work by which it serves the others. This is because we all have one baptism, one gospel, one faith, and are all Christians alike; for baptism, gospel, and faith alone make us spiritual and a Christian people.

But if a pope or bishop anoints, tonsures, ordains, consecrates, and prescribes garb different from that of the laity, he can perhaps thereby create a hypocrite or an anointed priestling, but he can never make anyone into a Christian or into a spiritual person by so doing. Accordingly, we are all consecrated priests through baptism, as St. Peter says in 1 Pet. 2[:9], "You are a royal priesthood and a priestly realm." And the Apocalypse says, "Thou hast made us to be priests and kings by thy blood" [Rev. 5:9-10]. For if we had no higher consecration than that which pope or bishop gives, such consecration by pope or bishop would never make a priest, and no one could say Mass or preach a sermon or give absolution.

Therefore, when a bishop consecrates it is nothing else than that in the place and in the name of the whole community, all members of which have the same power, he selects one person and charges him with exercising this power on behalf of the others. It is just as if ten brothers, all the sons and equal heirs of a king, were to choose one of their number to rule the inheritance for them: even though they are all kings and of equal power, one of them is charged with the responsibility of ruling. To put it still more clearly: suppose a group of earnest Christian laypeople were taken prisoner and set down in a desert without an episcopally ordained priest among them. And suppose they were to come to a common mind there and then in the desert and elect one of their number, whether he were married or not,[z] and charge him to baptize, say Mass, pronounce absolution, and preach the gospel. Such a man would be as truly a priest as if he had been ordained by all the bishops and popes in the world. This is why in cases of necessity anyone can baptize and give absolution.[14] This would be impossible if we were not all

14. On emergency baptism see, e.g., the bull *Exultate Deo* (1439), which decreed that in case of necessity anyone, "not only a priest or deacon but also a woman or, indeed, even a pagan or a heretic, has the power to baptize" (Carl Mirbt and Kurt Aland, eds. *Quellen zur Geschichte des Papsttums und des römischen Katholozismus*, 6th ed. (Tübingen: Mohr Siebeck, 1967), 485, no. 774, §10). The idea that in an emergency when no priest is available an ordinary layperson can hear confession and pronounce absolution can be traced to a statement of St. Augustine (354–430) that was incorporated into the *Decretum Gratiani* (cf. following note); Friedberg 1:1374.

z   The word here translated as "married," *ehelich*, can also mean "of legitimate birth." Canon law made both marriage and illegitimate birth a disqualification for ordination.

priests. Through canon law[15] the Romanists have almost destroyed and made unknown the wondrous grace and authority of baptism and Christian status. In times gone by, Christians used to choose their bishops and priests in this way from among their own number, and they were confirmed in their office by the other bishops without all the fuss that goes on nowadays. St. Augustine, Ambrose, and Cyprian each became [a bishop in this way].[16]

Since those who exercise secular authority have been baptized with the same baptism, and have the same faith and the same gospel as the rest of us, we must admit that they are priests and bishops, and we must regard their office as one that has a proper place in the Christian community and is useful to it. For whoever has crawled out of the water of baptism can boast that he is already a consecrated priest, bishop, and pope, even though it is not seemly that just anybody should exercise such an office. Because we are all priests of equal standing, no one must push himself forward and take it upon himself, without our consent and election, to do that for which we all have equal authority. For no one dare take upon himself what is common to all without the authority and consent of the community. And should it happen that someone chosen for such office were deposed for abuse of it, he would then be exactly what he was before. Therefore, a priest in Christendom is nothing else but an officeholder. As long as he holds office, he takes precedence; where he is deposed, he is a peasant or a townsman like anybody else. Indeed, a priest is never a priest when he is deposed. But now the Romanists have invented *characteres indelebiles* and blather that a deposed priest is nevertheless something different from a mere layman. They fancy that a priest can never be anything other than a priest, or ever become a layman.[17] All this is just contrived talk and human law.

It follows from this that there is no true, basic difference between laymen and priests, princes and bishops, or (as they say) between spiritual and secular, except that of office and work, and not that of status. For they are all of spiritual status, all are truly priests, bishops, and popes. But they do not

15. The term Luther uses here (and elsewhere) is *das geystlich recht* ("spiritual law"), a term that refers to church law as codified in the later medieval period into what is now known as the *Corpus Iuris Canonici*. Of the five collections that make up the *Corpus*, Luther referred most often to the two oldest: the *Decretum Gratiani* (c. 1140), and the *Decretals*, i.e., the *Liber Decretalium Gregorii IX* (1234). His attitude toward canon law was ambiguous. On the one hand, he hated it as the embodiment in law of papal tyranny. On the other hand, he found in it much useful evidence about the wholesome practices and teachings of the ancient church, and he became adroit at citing it to prove his contention that the "Romanists" ignored their own law when it suited their interests to do so. (On 10 December 1520 Luther burned a copy of canon law along with the papal bull of excommunication.)

16. St. Augustine, bishop of Hippo (354-430); St. Ambrose, bishop of Milan (c. 340-397); St. Cyprian, bishop of Carthage (d. 258).

17. The doctrine that ordination impresses on the soul an indelible mark that distinguishes the recipient from all those who have not received it was given authoritative formulation in the 1439 bull *Exultate Deo* of Pope Eugene IV (1383-1447); see Mirbt-Aland 484-85, no. 774, §9. Thus, a man in orders could cease functioning as a priest, but he could never again be a mere layman.

all have the same work to do, just as priests and monks do not all have exactly the same work. This is the teaching of St. Paul in Rom. 12[:4-5] and 1 Cor. 12[:12] and in 1 Pet. 2[:9], as I have said above, namely, that we are all one body of Christ the Head, and all members one of another. Christ has neither two bodies nor two kinds of body, one secular and the other spiritual. There is but one head and one body.

Therefore, just as those who are now called "spiritual," that is, priests, bishops, or popes, are neither different from other Christians nor superior to them, except that they are charged with the administration of the word of God and the sacraments, which is their work and office, so it is with secular government, which has the sword and rod in hand to punish the wicked and protect the good. A cobbler, a blacksmith, a peasant—each has the work and office of his trade, and yet they are all alike consecrated priests and bishops, and everyone should benefit and serve everyone else by means of their own work or office, so that in this way many kinds of work may be done for the bodily and spiritual welfare of the community, just as all the members of the body serve one another [1 Cor. 12:14-26].

Now consider how Christian the decree is which says that the secular power is not above the "spiritual estate" and has no right to punish it.[18] That is as much as to say that the hand should not help the eye when it suffers pain. Is it not unnatural, not to mention un-Christian, that one member should not help another and prevent its destruction? In fact, the more honorable the member, the more the others ought to help. I say therefore that since secular authority is ordained of God to punish the wicked and protect the good, it should be left free to perform its office in the whole body of Christendom without restriction and without respect to persons, whether it affects pope, bishops, priests, monks, nuns, or anyone else. If it were sufficient for the purpose of preventing secular authority from doing its work to say that among Christian offices it is inferior to that of preacher, confessor, or anyone of spiritual status, one would also have to prevent tailors, cobblers, stonemasons, carpenters, cooks, innkeepers, farmers, and the practitioners of all other secu-

18. The claim that spiritual authority was superior to all secular authority and not subject to correction by it was classically formulated in the 1302 bull *Unam sanctam* of Boniface VIII (c. 1235-1303). An important corollary of this view was the claim that clergymen had the *privilegium fori*, i.e., that they were exempt from the jurisdiction of the secular courts, even when charged with secular crimes. See nn. 21, 22 below.

lar trades from providing pope, bishops, priests, and monks with shoes, clothes, house, meat, and drink, as well as from paying them any tribute. But if these laypeople are allowed to do their proper work without restriction, what then are the Romanist scribes[19] doing with their own laws, which exempt them from the jurisdiction of secular Christian authority? It is just so that they can be free to do evil and fulfill what St. Peter said: "False teachers will rise up among you who will deceive you, and with their false and fanciful talk, they will take advantage of you" [2 Pet. 2:1-3].

For these reasons, Christian secular authority ought to exercise its office without hindrance, regardless of whether it is pope, bishop, or priest whom it affects. Whoever is guilty, let him suffer [punishment]. All that canon law has said to the contrary is the invention of Romanist presumption. For thus St. Paul says to all Christians, "Let every soul (I take that to mean the pope's soul also) be subject to governing authority, for it does not bear the sword in vain, but serves God by punishing the wicked and benefiting the good" [Rom. 13:1, 4]. St. Peter, too, says, "Be subject to all human ordinances for the sake of the Lord, who so wills it" [1 Pet. 2:13, 15]. He has also prophesied in 2 Pet. 2[:1] that such men would arise and despise secular government. This is exactly what has happened through canon law.

So I think this first paper wall is overthrown. Inasmuch as secular rule has become a part of the Christian body, it is part of the spiritual estate, even though its work is physical. Therefore, its work should extend without hindrance to all the members of the whole body, to punish and use force whenever guilt deserves or necessity demands, without regard to whether the culprit is pope, bishop, or priest. Let the Romanists hurl threats and bans as they like. That is why guilty priests, when they are handed over to secular law, are first deprived of their priestly dignities.[20] This would not be right unless the secular sword previously had had authority over these priests by divine right. Moreover, it is intolerable that in canon law so much importance is attached to the freedom, life, and property of the clergy,[21] as though the laity were not also as spiritual and as good Christians

19. An allusion to references in the Gospels to "scribes and Pharisees."

20. A clergyman found guilty of a secular crime by an ecclesiastical court was first deprived of his priestly office and then surrendered to the secular authorities for punishment.

21. In addition to the *privilegium fori* (see previous note), members of the clergy and religious orders enjoyed the *privilegium canonis*, according to which anyone who laid a hand on a clergyman or monk automatically incurred excommunication, the lifting of which was reserved to the pope. Canon law also declared that ecclesiastical persons and property were exempt from most of the general obligations (e.g., military service) and taxes required of laypeople (*privilegium immunitatis*).

22. An interdict banned the administration of the sacraments and other ecclesiastical rites (e.g., Christian burial) in a given jurisdiction, even an entire kingdom (as in the case of England, placed under interdict by Pope Innocent III [c. 1160–1216] in 1208). The use of interdict was not uncommon in the Middle Ages, but by 1500 its frequent use for trifling infractions of church law or clerical privilege was a common grievance of the laity against the clergy.

23. In his *Epitome* (see p. 370, n. 1), Sylvester Prierias had quoted this provision of canon law against Luther: "An undoubtedly legitimate pope cannot be lawfully deposed or judged by either a council or the entire world, even if he be so scandalous as to lead people with him *en masse* into the possession of the devil in hell." See WA 6:336.

as they, or did not also belong to the church. Why are your life and limb, your property and honor, so cheap and mine not, inasmuch as we are all Christians and have the same baptism, the same faith, the same Spirit, and all the rest? If a priest is murdered, the whole country is placed under interdict.[22] Why not when a peasant is murdered? How does this great difference come about between two men who are both Christians? It comes from the laws and fabrications of men.

It can, moreover, be no good spirit that has invented such exceptions and granted such license and impunity to sin. For if it is our duty to strive against the words and works of the devil and to drive him out in whatever way we can, as both Christ and his apostles command us, how have we come to the point that we have to do nothing and say nothing when the pope or his cohorts undertake devilish words and works? Ought we merely out of regard for these people allow the suppression of divine commandments and truth, which we have sworn in baptism to support with life and limb? Then we should have to answer for all the souls that would thereby be abandoned and led astray!

It must, therefore, have been the chief devil himself who said what is written in the canon law, that if the pope were so scandalously bad as to lead crowds of souls to the devil, still he could not be deposed.[23] At Rome they build on this accursed and devilish foundation, and think that we should let all the world go to the devil rather than resist their knavery. If the fact that one man is set over others were sufficient reason why he should not be punished, then no Christian could punish another, since Christ commanded that all people should esteem themselves as the lowliest and the least [Matt. 18:4].

Where sin is, there is no longer any shielding from punishment. St. Gregory writes that we are indeed all equal, but guilt makes a person inferior to others.[a] Now we see how the Romanists treat Christendom. They take away its freedom without any proof from Scripture, at their own whim. But God, as well as the apostles, made them subject to the

---

a   Pope Gregory the Great (c. 540–604), *Regula pastoralis* 2.6.

secular sword. It is to be feared that this is a game of the Antichrist,[24] or at any rate that his forerunner has appeared.

The second wall is still more loosely built and less substantial. [The Romanists] want to be the only masters of Holy Scripture, although they never learn a thing from the Bible all their life long. They assume the sole authority for themselves, and, quite unashamed, they play about with words before our very eyes, trying to persuade us that the pope cannot err in matters of faith, regardless of whether he is righteous or wicked.[25] Yet they cannot point to a single letter.[b] This is why so many heretical and un-Christian, even unnatural, ordinances stand in the canon law. But there is no need to talk about these ordinances at present. Since these Romanists think the Holy Spirit never leaves them, no matter how ignorant and wicked they are, they become bold and decree only what they want. And if what they claim were true, why have Holy Scripture at all? Of what use is Scripture? Let us burn the Scripture and be satisfied with the unlearned gentlemen at Rome who possess the Holy Spirit! And yet the Holy Spirit can be possessed only by upright hearts. If I had not read the words with my own eyes,[c] I would not have believed it possible for the devil to have made such stupid claims at Rome, and to have won supporters for them.

But so as not to fight them with mere words, we will quote the Scriptures. St. Paul says in 1 Cor. 14[:30], "If something better is revealed to anyone, though he is already sitting and listening to another in God's word, then the one who is speaking shall hold his peace and give place." What would be the point of this commandment if we were compelled to believe only the man who does the talking, or the man who is at the top? Even Christ said in John 6[:45] that all Christians shall be taught by God. If it were to happen that the pope and his cohorts were wicked and not true Christians, were not taught by God and were without understanding, and at the same time some obscure person had a right

24. Luther and his contemporaries believed the appearance of the Antichrist was prophesied in 2 Thess. 2:3-10; 1 John 2:18, 22; 4:3; and Revelation 13. It was precisely at this time that Luther's suspicion that the papacy was the Antichrist turned to conviction and was expressed publicly in his response to the *Epitome* of Prierias; see the introduction, p. 370, n. 1 and note d.

25. Papal infallibility did not finally become official doctrine of the Catholic Church until 1870. In Luther's day, it was an opinion that had long been vigorously asserted by champions of papal authority, particularly at the Curia in Rome, but was not universally accepted. In his attack on the *95 Theses*, for example, Sylvester Prierias had argued, without citing Scripture, that "whoever does not rely on the teaching of the Roman church and the supreme pontiff as an infallible rule of faith, from which even Holy Scripture draws its vigor and authority, is a heretic" (*D. Martini Lutheri Opera Latina varii argumenti*, vol. 1: *Scripta 1515–1518* [Frankfurt/Main: Heyder & Zimmer, 1865], 347. But in the wake of Luther's excommunication in 1521, there were many in Germany and elsewhere who did not believe that he was a heretic just because the pope said so.

b   I.e., to a single letter of Scripture to support their claim.
c   Luther is referring to the passage quoted in n. 25.

understanding, why should the people not follow that one? Has the pope not erred many times? Who would help Christendom when the pope erred if we did not have others[d] who had the Scriptures on their side and whom we could trust more than him?

Therefore, their claim that only the pope may interpret Scripture is an outrageous fancied fable. They cannot produce a single letter [of Scripture] to maintain that the interpretation of Scripture or the confirmation of its interpretation belongs to the pope alone. They themselves have usurped this power. And although they allege that this power was given to St. Peter when the keys were given him, it is clear enough that the keys were not given to Peter alone but to the whole community.[e] Further, the keys were not ordained for doctrine or government, but only for the binding or loosing of sin. Whatever else or whatever more they arrogate to themselves on the basis of the keys is a mere fabrication. But Christ's words to Peter, "I have prayed for you that your faith fail not" [Luke 22:32], cannot be applied to the pope, since the majority of the popes have been without faith, as they must themselves confess. Besides, it is not only for Peter that Christ prayed, but also for all apostles and Christians, as he says in John 17[:9, 20], "Father, I pray for those whom thou hast given me, and not for these only, but for all who believe on me through their word." Is that not clear enough?

Just think of it! The Romanists must admit that there are among us good Christians who have the true faith, spirit, understanding, word, and mind of Christ. Why, then, should we reject the word and understanding of good Christians and follow the pope, who has neither faith nor intelligence? To follow the pope would be to deny the whole faith as well as the Christian church. Again, if the article, "I believe in one holy Christian church," is correct, then the pope cannot be the only one who is right.[f] Otherwise, we would have

d   Singular in the original.

e   Matt. 16:19; 18:18; and John 20:23. See above, pp. 195–96 (*The Sacrament of Penance*, 1519). For the "Keys," see above, p. 37, n. 36.

f   Citing the Nicene Creed, according to the standard German translation.

to pray, "I believe in the pope at Rome." This would reduce the Christian church to one man, and be nothing else than a devilish and hellish error.

Besides, if we are all priests, as was said above,[g] and all have one faith, one gospel, one sacrament, why should we not also have the power to test and judge what is right or wrong in matters of faith? What becomes of Paul's words in 1 Cor. 2[:15], "A spiritual person judges all things and yet is judged by no one"? And 2 Cor. 4[:13], "We all have one spirit of faith"? Why, then, should not we perceive what is consistent with faith and what is not, just as well as an unbelieving pope does?

We ought to become bold and free on the authority of all these texts, and many others. We ought not to allow the Spirit of freedom (Paul's appellation [2 Cor. 3:17]) to be frightened off by the fabrications of the popes but ought rather to march boldly forward and test all that they do or leave undone by our faithful understanding of the Scriptures. We must compel the Romanists to follow not their own interpretation but the better one. Long ago Abraham had to listen to Sarah, although she was in more complete subjection to him than we are to anyone on earth [Gen. 21:12]. And Balaam's donkey was wiser than the prophet himself [Num. 22:21-35]. If God spoke then through a donkey against a prophet, why should he not be able even now to speak through a righteous person against the pope? Similarly, St. Paul rebukes St. Peter as someone in error in Gal. 2[:11-12]. Therefore, it is the duty of every Christian to espouse the cause of the faith, to understand and defend it, and to denounce every error.

The third wall[26] falls of itself once the first two are down. For when the pope acts contrary to the Scriptures, it is our duty to stand by the Scriptures, to reprove him, and to constrain him, according to the word of Christ, Matthew 18[:15-17], "If your brother sins against you, go and tell it to him, between you and him alone; if he does not listen to you, then take one or two others with you; if he does not

26. See p. 381 (first wall) and p. 387 (second wall).

g   See p. 383f.

listen to them, tell it to the church; if he does not listen to the church, consider him a heathen." Here every member is commanded to care for every other. How much more should we do this when the member that does evil is responsible for the government of the church, and by that one's evildoing is the cause of much harm and offense to the rest. But if I am to accuse such a person before the church, I must naturally call the church together.

[The Romanists] have no basis in Scripture for their claim that the pope alone has the right to call or confirm a council.[27] It is just their own law, and it is only valid as long as it is not harmful to Christendom or contrary to the laws of God. But if the pope deserves punishment, this law ceases to be valid, for it is harmful to Christendom not to punish him by authority of a council.

Thus we read in Acts 15 that it was not St. Peter who called the Apostolic Council but the apostles and elders. If then that right had belonged to St. Peter alone, the council would not have been a Christian council, but a heretical *conciliabulum*.[h] Even the Council of Nicaea, the most famous of all councils, was neither called nor confirmed by the bishop of Rome, but by the emperor Constantine.[28] Many other emperors after him have done the same, and yet these councils were the most Christian of all.[29] But if the pope alone has the right to convene councils, then these councils would all have been heretical. Further, when I examine the councils the pope did summon, I find that they did nothing of special importance.

Therefore, when necessity demands it, and the pope is an offense to Christendom, the first one who is able should, as true members of the whole body, do what can be done to bring about a truly free council. No one can do this so well as the secular authorities, especially since they are also fellow-Christians, fellow-priests, fellow-participants in spiritual authority, sharing power over all things. Whenever it is necessary or profitable, they ought to exercise the office and work that they have received from God over everyone.

27. The claim, asserted in several decrees of canon law, had been advanced against Luther by Prierias in his *Epitome*: "[W]hen there is one undisputed pontiff, it belongs to him alone to call a council." Moreover, "the decrees of councils neither bind nor constrain unless they are confirmed by the authority of the Roman pontiff" (WA 6:335).

28. The Council of Nicaea (325), the first general council, was called by Emperor Constantine (c. 272–337) to deal with the Arian Controversy.

29. Besides Nicaea, there were the councils of Constantinople (381), Ephesus (431), and Chalcedon (451). More recently, Emperor Maximilian I and King Louis XII (1462–1515) of France had convoked the Second Council of Pisa (1511), but Pope Julius II countered by summoning the Fifth Lateran Council to Rome (1512).

---

h   I.e., a miserable little invalid gathering rather than a true council.

Would it not be unnatural if a fire broke out in a city and everybody were to stand by and let it burn on and on and consume everything that could burn because nobody had the authority of the mayor, or because, perhaps, the fire broke out in the mayor's house? In such a situation is it not the duty of every citizen to rouse and summon the rest? How much more should this be done in the spiritual city of Christ if a fire of offense breaks out, whether in the pope's government or anywhere else! The same argument holds if an enemy were to attack a city. The person who first rouses the others deserves honor and gratitude. Why, then, should that person not deserve honor who makes known the presence of the enemy from hell and rouses Christian people and calls them together?

All their boasting about an authority that dare not be opposed amounts to nothing at all. Nobody in Christendom has authority to do injury or to forbid the resisting of injury. There is no authority in the church except to foster improvement. Therefore, if the pope were to use his authority to prevent the calling of a free council, thereby preventing the improvement of the church, we should have regard neither for him nor for his authority. And if he were to hurl his bans and thunderbolts, we should despise his conduct as that of a madman, and we should instead ban him and drive him out as best we can, relying completely upon God. For his presumptuous authority is nothing, nor does he possess it. He is quickly defeated by a single text of Scripture, where Paul says to the Corinthians, "God has given us authority not to ruin Christendom, but to build it up" [2 Cor. 10:8]. Who will leap over the hurdle of this text? It is the power of the devil and of Antichrist, which resists the things that serve to build up Christendom. Such power is not to be obeyed, but rather resisted with life, property, and with all our might and main.

Even though a miracle were to be performed against secular authority on the pope's behalf, or if somebody were struck down by the plague—which they boast has sometimes happened—it should be considered as nothing but the work of the devil designed to destroy our faith in God.

Statue of Emperor Constantine.

Christ foretold this in Matt. 24[:24], "False Christs and false prophets shall come in my name, who shall perform signs and miracles in order to deceive even the elect." And Paul says in 2 Thess. 2[:9] that Antichrist shall, through the power of Satan, be mighty in false miracles.

Let us, therefore, hold fast to this: Christian authority can do nothing against Christ. As St. Paul says, "We can do nothing against Christ, only for Christ" [2 Cor. 13:8]. But if an authority does anything against Christ, then it is that of the Antichrist and the devil, even if it were to rain and hail miracles and plagues. Miracles and plagues prove nothing, especially in these evil latter days. The whole of Scripture foretells such false miracles. This is why we must cling to the word of God with firm faith, and then the devil will soon drop his miracles!

With this I hope that all these wicked and lying terrors, with which the Romanists have long intimidated and dulled our consciences, have been overcome and that they, just like all of us, shall be made subject to the sword. For they have no right to interpret Scripture merely on their own authority and without learning. They have no authority to prevent a council, much less at their mere whim to put it under obligation, impose conditions on it, or deprive it of its freedom. When they do such things, they are truly in the fellowship of Antichrist and the devil. They have nothing at all of Christ except the name.

Let us now look at the matters that ought to be properly dealt with in councils, matters with which popes, cardinals, bishops, and all scholars ought properly to be occupied day and night if they loved Christ and his church. But if this is not the case, let ordinary people[i] and the secular authorities take action,[j] without regard to papal bans and fulminations, for [suffering under] an unjust ban is better than ten just and proper absolutions, and [trusting] one unjust,

Papal coat of arms showing a triple-crowned tiara.

---

i   Luther's word is *der hauff* (literally, "the crowd," i.e., ordinary people without ecclesiastical office).

j   I.e., convoke a council and do whatever else they can to restore health to the church.

improper absolution is worse than ten just bans. Therefore, let us awake, dear Germans, and fear God more than mortals [Acts 5:29], lest we suffer the same fate of all the poor souls who are so lamentably lost through the shameless, devilish rule of the Romanists, and the devil grow stronger every day—as if it were possible that such a hellish regime could grow any worse, something that I can neither conceive nor believe.

First. It is horrible and shocking to see the head of Christendom, who boasts that he is the vicar of Christ and successor of St. Peter, going about in such a worldly and ostentatious style that neither king nor emperor can equal or approach him. He claims the title of "most holy" and "most spiritual," and yet he is worldlier than the world itself. He wears a triple crown, whereas the highest monarchs wear but one.[30] If that is like the poverty of Christ and of St. Peter, then it is a new and strange kind of likeness! When anybody says anything against it, [the Romanists] bleat, "Heresy!" They refuse to hear how un-Christian and ungodly all this is. In my opinion, if the pope were to pray to God with tears, he would have to lay aside his triple crown, for the God we worship cannot put up with pride. In fact, the pope's office should be nothing else but to weep and pray for Christendom and to set an example of utter humility.

Be that as it may, this kind of splendor is offensive, and the pope is bound for the sake of his own salvation to set it aside. It was for this reason that St. Paul said, "Abstain from all practices which give offense" [1 Thess. 5:22], and in Rom. 12[:17], "We should do good, not only in the sight of God, but also in the sight of all people." An ordinary bishop's mitre ought to be good enough for the pope. It is in wisdom and holiness that he should be above his fellows. He ought to leave the crown of pride to Antichrist, as his predecessors did centuries ago. The Romanists say he is a lord of the earth. That is a lie! For Christ, whose vicar and vicegerent he claims to be, said to Pilate, "My kingdom is not of this world" [John 18:36]. No vicar's rule can go beyond that of his lord. Moreover, he is not the vicar of Christ glorified but of Christ crucified. As Paul says, "I was determined

30. The tiara or triple crown, the papal headdress on nonliturgical occasions, was first used in the fourteenth century. The symbolism of the three layers of the crown was variously interpreted, but it undoubtedly included the assertion of the pope's elevation above all secular authority as well as his headship of the church.

to know nothing among you save Christ, and him only as the crucified" [1 Cor. 2:2], and in Phil. 2[:5-7], "This is how you should regard yourselves, as you see in Christ, who emptied himself and took upon himself the form of a servant." Or again in 1 Cor. 1[:23], "We preach Christ, the crucified." Now the Romanists make the pope a vicar of the glorified Christ in heaven, and some of them have allowed the devil to rule them so completely that they have maintained that the pope is above the angels in heaven and has them at his command.[31] These are certainly the proper works of the real Antichrist.

Second. Of what use to Christendom are those people called cardinals? I shall tell you. Italy and Germany have many rich monasteries, foundations,[k] benefices, and livings. No better way has been discovered of bringing all these to Rome than by creating cardinals and giving them bishoprics, monasteries, and prelacies for their own use and so overthrowing the worship of God. You can see that Italy is now almost a wilderness: monasteries in ruins, bishoprics despoiled, the prelacies and the revenues of all the churches drawn to Rome, cities decayed, land and people ruined because services are no longer held and the word of God is not preached. And why? Because the cardinals must have the income! No Turk[32] could have devastated Italy and suppressed the worship of God so effectively!

Now that Italy is sucked dry, the Romanists are coming into Germany.[l] They have made a gentle beginning. But let us keep our eyes open! Germany shall soon be like Italy. We have some cardinals already. The "drunken Germans" are not supposed to understand what the Romanists are up to until there is not a bishopric, a monastery, a parish, a benefice, not a single penny left. Antichrist must seize the treasures of the earth, as it is prophesied [Dan. 11:39, 43]. It works like this: they skim the cream off the bishoprics, monasteries, and benefices, and because they do not yet ven-

---

31. Cf. LW 32:74-75. This claim was advanced by Augustinus de Ancona (known as Augustinus Triumphans [1243-1328]) in Quaestio 18 of his *Summa de potestate ecclesiastica*, 1326 (first printed at Augsburg in 1473). See Blasius Ministeri, "De vita et operibus Augustine de Ancona, O.E.S.A. (d. 1328)," *Analecta Augustiniana* 22 (1953): 115, 156.

32. Luther's term for adherents of Islam, who were familiar to sixteenth-century Europeans primarily as Muslims from the Ottoman Turkish Empire. Besides being his word for subjects of the Ottoman Turkish Empire, "Turk" was Luther's word for "Muslim." Islam was familiar to sixteenth-century Europeans primarily via their confrontation with the Ottoman Turks, who were long a military threat on the eastern borders of the Holy Roman Empire as well as in the Mediterranean.

---

k   German: *Stift*. This refers to university foundations and the collegiate foundations of cathedrals.

l   Cf. *Treatise on Good Works*, above, p. 340f.

ture to put them all to shameful use, as they have done in Italy, they in the meantime practice their holy cunning and couple together ten or twenty prelacies. They then tear off a little piece each year so as to make quite a tidy sum after all. The provostship of Würzburg yields a thousand gulden; that of Bamberg also yields a sum, [as do] Mainz, Trier, and others. In this way, one thousand or ten thousand gulden may be collected, so that a cardinal could live like a wealthy monarch at Rome.

When we have gotten used to that, we shall appoint thirty or forty cardinals in one day.[33] We shall give to one of them the Münchenberg at Bamberg,[m] along with the bishopric of Würzburg, with a few rich benefices attached to them, until churches and cities are destitute, and then we shall say, "We are Christ's vicars, and shepherds of Christ's sheep. The foolish, drunken Germans will just have to put up with it."

My advice, however, is to make fewer cardinals, or to let the pope support them at his own expense. Twelve of them would be enough, and each of them might have an income of a thousand gulden.[34] How is it that we Germans must put up with such robbery and extortion of our goods at the hands of the pope? If the kingdom of France has prevented it, why do we Germans let them make such fools and apes of us?[35] We could put up with all this if they stole only our property, but they lay waste to the churches in so doing, rob Christ's sheep of their true shepherds, and debase the worship and word of God. If there were not a single cardinal, the church would not perish. The cardinals do nothing to serve Christendom. They are only interested in the money side of bishoprics and prelacies, and they wrangle about them just as any thief might do.

Third. If ninety-nine percent of the papal court were abolished and only one percent kept, it would still be large enough to give answers in matters of faith. Today, however, there is such a swarm of parasites in that place called Rome, all of them boasting that they belong to the pope, that not even Babylon saw the likes of it. There are more than three

33. On 1 July 1517, Pope Leo X (1475–1521) named thirty-one cardinals, the largest number ever created in a single consistory until 1946. At the end of Leo's reign, the total number of cardinals was forty-eight, seventeen more than it had been at the time of his election in 1513, but only three more than it had been at the time of the election of Julius II in 1503.

34. It was a common complaint that the College of Cardinals was too large, its size fed more by the income derived from the fees charged for an appointment to it than by the needs of the church. The fifteenth-century reform councils of Constance and Basel had wanted the total number fixed at twenty-four. The actual number at this time tended to hover at around twice that (see n. 33). The idea that the cardinals should be assigned a fixed income rather than endowed with benefices was also a common suggestion in the literature for church reform. The Council of Constance recommended an income of three to four thousand gulden.

35. In 1438 King Charles VIII (1470–1498) of France presided over a synod of French clergy and nobility at Bourges that adopted the so-called

---

m   I.e., the Michaelsberg Abbey in Bamberg.

Pragmatic Sanction, which applied to France some of the reform decrees of the Council of Basel. In effect, the Pragmatic Sanction took control over the election of bishops, abbots, and other benefice holders in France away from the pope and bestowed it on the crown, thus severely reducing the income derived from such appointments by the pope or his nonresident appointees. The payment of annates (see n. 37) to the pope was forbidden. In 1516 Pope Leo X and King Francis I (1494–1547) concluded the Concordat of Bologna, which replaced the Pragmatic Sanction but kept many of its provisions. The right of nomination to bishoprics and other high offices was expressly reserved to the crown, the pope retaining the right to withhold confirmation from appointments that violated canonical requirements. The matter of annates, however, was passed over in complete silence, which meant that the pope was tacitly given permission to collect them again. In Germany, relations between the pope and the German church were regulated by the Concordat of Vienna, concluded by Pope Nicholas V (1397–1455) and Emperor Frederick III (1415–1493) in 1448. By its terms, the pope had much greater freedom in appointments to ecclesiastical office and in collection revenues.

36. The papal court, or Curia, consisted of all the officials engaged in conduct of papal business as well as the pope's personal "household." According to a list published at Rome in 1545, there were in that year 949 curial positions that were available for the one-time payment of a fee. This

thousand papal secretaries alone. Who could count the other officials? There are so many offices that one could scarcely count them.[36] These are all the people lying in wait for the endowments and benefices of Germany as wolves lie in wait for sheep. I believe that Germany now gives much more to the pope at Rome than it used to give to the emperors in ancient times. In fact, some have estimated that more than three hundred thousand gulden a year find their way from Germany to Rome.[n] This money serves no use or purpose. We get nothing for it except scorn and contempt. And we still go on wondering why princes and nobles, cities and endowments, land and people, grow poor. We ought to marvel that we have anything left to eat!

Since we have now come to the heart of the matter, we will pause a little and let it be seen that the Germans are not quite such crass fools that they know nothing about or do not understand the sharp practices of the Romanists. I do not here complain that God's command and Christian law are despised at Rome, for things are not going so well throughout Christendom, especially in Rome, that we may complain of such exalted matters. Nor do I complain that natural law, or secular law, or even reason count for nothing. My complaint goes deeper than that. I complain that the Romanists do not keep their own fabricated canon law, even though it is in fact plain tyranny, avarice, and temporal splendor rather than genuine law. This we shall see.

In former times, German emperors and princes permitted the pope to receive annates from all the benefices of the German nation. This sum amounts to one-half of the revenue of the first year from every single benefice.[37] This permission was given, however, so that by means of these large sums of money the pope might raise funds to fight against the Turks and infidels in defense of Christendom, and, so that the burden of war might not rest too heavily upon the nobility, the clergy too should contribute something toward it. The popes have so far used the splendid and simple devotion of the German people—they have received this money for more

n   See RTA 2:675, par. 11.

than a hundred years and have now made it an obligatory tax and tribute, but they have not only amassed no money [for this defense], they have used it to endow many posts and positions at Rome and to provide salaries for these posts, as though annates were a fixed rent.

When they pretend that they are about to fight the Turks, they send out emissaries to raise money. They often issue an indulgence on the same pretext of fighting the Turks. They think that those half-witted Germans will always be gullible, stupid fools, and will just keep handing over money to them to satisfy their unspeakable greed. And they think this even though it is public knowledge that not a cent of the annates, or of the indulgence money, or of all the rest, is spent to fight the Turks. It all goes into their bottomless moneybag. They lie and deceive. They make laws and they make agreements with us, but they do not intend to keep a single letter of them. Yet all this is done in the holy names of Christ and St. Peter.

In this matter, the German nation, bishops and princes, should now consider that they, too, are Christians. They should govern and protect the physical and spiritual goods of the people entrusted to them and defend them against these rapacious wolves who, dressed in sheep's clothing, pretend to be shepherds and rulers.[o] And since annates have been so shockingly abused, and not even kept for their original agreed purpose, [the bishops and princes] should not allow their land and people to be so pitilessly robbed and ruined contrary to all law. By decree either of the emperor or of the whole nation[p] the annates should either be kept here at home or else abolished. Since the Romanists do not abide by their agreement, they have no right to the annates. Therefore, the bishops and princes are responsible for punishing such thievery and robbery, or even preventing it, as the law requires.

In such a matter, they ought to help the pope and strengthen his hand. Perhaps he is too weak to prevent such

number did not include the members of the papal household or the officials responsible for the government of the city of Rome and the papal states. See Benrath, 88, n. 18; 95–96, n. 36.

37. *Annates* consisted of the first year's revenue of an ecclesiastical benefice (or a specified portion of that revenue) paid to the papal treasury in return for appointment to that benefice. The rate of half the annual revenue was set by Pope John XXII (1244–1334) in 1317. It was an onerous tribute and much resented. The Council of Constance (1415) limited the payment of annates to bishoprics, abbacies, and other benefices with an income of more than twenty-four gulden, a rule that was applied to Germany in the Concordat of Vienna (1448).

o   Cf. Matt. 7:15.
p   That is, by decree of the imperial diet.

38. Ever since the early fourteenth century, popes had claimed the authority to reserve to themselves the right of appointment to all ecclesiastical benefices, a right that might in specific cases be graciously conceded to others (Friedberg 2:1259–61). Abolished in France, "reservations" were still valid in Germany. The Concordat of Vienna (1448) provided for the free election of bishops and abbots, subject to confirmation by the pope, who could object to persons deemed unsuitable. If the election were found to violate canon law, the pope was to provide a candidate. In the case of canonries and other benefices below those of highest rank, those that fell vacant in the even-numbered months of the year were reserved for appointment by the pope. In the odd-numbered months, local authorities exercised their right of election.

39. Charles V (1500–1558) was Holy Roman Emperor from 1519 to 1556. His empire included Spain and the Habsburg Empire that extended across Europe from Spain and the Netherlands to Austria and the Kingdom of Naples.

40. The ecclesiastical jurisdiction of the Holy Catholic Church in Rome.

abuse single-handedly. Or, in those cases where he wants to defend and maintain this state of affairs, they ought to resist him and protect themselves from him as they would from a wolf or a tyrant, for he has no authority to do evil or defend it. Even if it were ever desirable to raise such funds to fight the Turks, we ought to have at least enough sense to see that the German nation could better manage these funds than the pope. The German nation itself has enough people to wage war if the money is available. It is the same with annates as it has been with many other Romanist schemes.

Then, too, the year has been so divided between the pope and the ruling bishops and chapters that the pope has six months in the year (every other month) in which to bestow the benefices that become vacant in his months. In this way, almost all the best benefices have fallen into the hands of Rome, especially the very best prebends and dignities.[38] And when they once fall into the hands of Rome, they never come out of them again, though a vacancy may never occur again in the pope's month. In this way the chapters are short-changed. This is plain robbery, and the intention is to let nothing escape. Therefore, it is high time to abolish the "papal months" altogether. Everything that has been taken to Rome in this way must be restored. The princes and nobles ought to take steps for the restitution of the stolen property, punish the thieves, and strip the privilege of those who have abused that privilege. If it is binding and valid for the pope on the day after his election to make regulations and laws in his chancellery by which our endowed chapters and livings are stolen from us—a thing he has absolutely no right to do—then it should be still more valid for Emperor Charles,[39] on the day after his coronation, to make rules and laws that not another benefice or living in all Germany should be allowed to pass into the hands of Rome by means of the "papal months." The livings that have already fallen into the hands of Rome should be restored and redeemed from these Romanist robbers. Charles V has the right to do this by virtue of his authority as ruler.

But now this Romanist See[40] of avarice and robbery has not had the patience to wait for the time when all the benefices would fall to it one by one through this device of the "papal months." Rather, urged on by its insatiable appetite to get them all in its hands as speedily as possible, the Romanist See has devised a scheme whereby, in addition to the "annates" and "papal months," the benefices and livings should fall to Rome in three ways.[q]

First, if anyone who holds a "free" living[r] should die in Rome or on a journey to Rome, his living becomes the property in perpetuity of the Romanist—I ought to say roguish—See. But the Romanists do not want to be called robbers on this account, though they are guilty of robbery of a kind never heard of or read about before.

Second, if anyone belonging to the household of the pope or cardinals holds or takes over a benefice, or if anyone who had previously held a benefice subsequently enters the household of the pope or cardinals, [his living becomes the property in perpetuity of the Romanist See]. But who can count the household of the pope and cardinals? If he only goes on a pleasure ride, the pope takes with him three or four thousand on mules, in disdain of all emperors and kings! Christ and St. Peter went on foot so that their successors might have all the more pomp and splendor. Now Avarice has cleverly thought out another scheme, and arranges it so that many even outside Rome have the name "member of the papal household" just as if they were in Rome. This is done for the sole purpose that, by the simple use of that pernicious phrase "member of the pope's household," all benefices may be brought to Rome and bound there for all time. Are not these vexatious and devilish little inventions? Let us beware! Soon Mainz, Magdeburg, and Halberstadt will quietly slip into the hands of Rome, and then the cardinalate will cost a pretty penny![41] After that they will make all the German bishops cardinals, and then there will be nothing left.

Portrait of Holy Roman Emperor, Charles V.

41. The reference is to the accumulation of bishoprics in the hands of Albrecht von Brandenburg (1490–1545), who in 1513 became archbishop of Magdeburg and administrator of the bishopric of Halberstadt, and in the following year archbishop-elector of Mainz. In 1518 he was made cardinal. The need to raise money to pay the enormous fees for the dispensations from the canonical ban on such accumulation of benefices was in part behind the sale of indulgences by Johann Tetzel (c. 1460–1519). Luther objected to this indulgence in the *95 Theses* but was unaware of Albrecht's financial dealings. See above, p. 17f.

---

q   Here Luther summarizes provisions of the Concordat of Vienna.

r   I.e., one not previously subject to appointment by the pope.

Third, when a dispute has started at Rome over a benefice, [it reverts to Roman control]. In my opinion this is the commonest and widest road for bringing livings into the hands of Rome. Even when there is no real dispute, countless knaves will be found at Rome who will unearth one and snatch the benefices at will. Thus many a good priest must lose his living or pay a sum of money to avoid having his benefice disputed. Such a living, rightly or wrongly contested, becomes the property of the Roman See forever. It would be no wonder if God were to rain fire and brimstone from heaven and sink Rome into the abyss, as he did Sodom and Gomorrah of old [Gen. 19:24]. Why should there be a pope in Christendom if his power is used for nothing else than for such gross wickedness and to protect and practice it? O noble princes and lords, how long will you leave your lands and your people naked and exposed to such ravenous wolves?

Since even these practices were not enough, and Avarice grew impatient at the long time it took to seize all the bishoprics, my Lord Avarice devised the fiction that the bishoprics should be nominally abroad but that their origin and foundation is at Rome. Furthermore, no bishop can be confirmed unless he pays a huge sum for his pallium and binds himself with solemn oaths to the personal service of the pope.[42] That explains why no bishop dares to act against the pope. That is what the Romanists were seeking when they imposed the oath [of allegiance]. It also explains why all the richest bishoprics have fallen into debt and ruin. I am told that Mainz pays twenty thousand gulden.[s] That is the Romanists all over! To be sure, they decreed a long time ago in canon law that the pallium should be given without cost, that the number in the pope's household be reduced, disputes lessened, and the chapters and bishops allowed their liberty. But this did not bring in money. So they turned over a new leaf and have taken all authority away from the bishops and chapters. These sit there like ciphers and have neither office nor authority nor work. Everything is con-

42. The pallium, a woolen shoulder cape that had to be secured from Rome, was the emblem of the office of archbishop as well as a symbol of his close ties to the papacy. A newly elected archbishop was required to acquire the pallium within three months of his election. In the early history of the church, it had been granted free of charge, but by Luther's day it had long since become an extremely expensive acquisition.

s   Elsewhere Luther put the price at thirty thousand; see LW 39:60 (*On the Papacy in Rome*).

trolled by those arch-villains at Rome, almost right down to the office of sexton and bell ringer. Every dispute is called to Rome, and everyone does just as he pleases, under cover of the pope's authority.

What has happened in this very year? The bishop of Strasbourg wanted to govern his chapter properly and reform it in matters of worship. With this end in view, he established certain godly and Christian regulations. But our dear friend the pope and the Holy Roman See wrecked and damned this holy and spiritual ordinance, all at the instigation of the priests.[43] This is called feeding the sheep of Christ! That is how priests are strengthened against their own bishop, and how their disobedience to divine law is protected! Antichrist himself, I hope, will not dare to shame God so openly. There is your pope for you! Just as you have always wanted! Why did the pope do this? Ah! If one church were reformed, that would be a dangerous breakthrough. Rome might have to follow suit. Therefore, it is better that no priest be allowed to get along with another and, as we have grown accustomed to seeing right up to the present day, that kings and princes should be set at odds. It is better to flood the world with Christian blood, lest the unity of Christians compel the Holy Roman See to reform itself!

So far we have been considering how they deal with benefices that become vacant and are unoccupied. But for tender-hearted Avarice the vacancies are too few. Therefore, he has kept a very close watch even on those benefices still occupied by their incumbents, so that these too can be made vacant, even though they are not now vacant. He does this in several ways.

First, Avarice lies in wait where fat prebends or bishoprics are held by an old or sick man, or even by one with an alleged disability. The Holy See then provides a coadjutor, that is, an assistant, to an incumbent of this kind. This is done without the holder's consent or permission, and for the benefit of the coadjutor, because he is a member of the pope's "household," or because he has paid for it, or has otherwise earned it by some sort of service to Rome. In this case, the free rights of the chapter or the rights of the incumbent

43. Although he became a determined opponent of the Reformation, Wilhelm III, Count of Honstein (c. 1470–1541), bishop of Strasbourg from 1506 to 1541, had a long history of failed attempts to reform the clergy of his diocese. It is not clear what particular event Luther is referring to here, but he appears to have learned of it from Georg Spalatin; see WA Br 2:130, 20.

are disregarded, and the whole thing falls into the hands of Rome.

Second, there is the little word *commenda*.[44] This means the pope puts a cardinal, or another of his underlings, in charge of a rich, prosperous monastery, just as if I were to give you a hundred gulden to keep. This does not mean to give the monastery or bestow it. Nor does it mean abolishing it or the divine service. It means quite simply to give it into his keeping. Not that he to whom it is entrusted is to care for it or build it up, but he is to drive out the incumbent, receive the goods and revenues, and install some apostate, renegade monk or another,[45] who accepts five or six gulden a year and sits all day long in the church selling pictures and images to the pilgrims, so that neither prayers nor Masses are said in that place anymore. If this were to be called destroying monasteries and abolishing the worship of God, then the pope would have to be called a destroyer of Christendom and an abolisher of divine worship. He certainly does well at it! But this would be harsh language for Rome, so they have to call it a "*commenda*," or an entrusting for taking over the charge of the monastery. The pope can make "*commenda*" of four or more of these monasteries in one year, any single one of which may have an income of more than six thousand gulden. This is how the Romanists increase the worship of God and maintain the monasteries! Even the Germans are beginning to find that out!

Third, there are some benefices they call *incompatabilia*,[46] which, according to the ordinances of canon law, cannot be held at the same time, such as two parishes, two bishoprics, and the like. In these cases, the Holy Roman See of Avarice evades canon law by making glosses to its own advantage,[47] called *unio* and *incorporatio*. This means that the pope incorporates many *incompatabilia* into one single unit, so that each is a part of every other, and all of them together are looked upon as one benefice. They are then no longer *incompatabilia*, and the holy canon law is satisfied because it is no longer binding, except upon those who do not buy these glosses from the pope or his *datarius*.[48] The *unio*, that is, the uniting, is very similar. The pope combines many such

---

44. To be awarded a benefice *in commendam* was to be assigned the income from it without being obligated to perform the spiritual office that went with it (which would usually be assigned to a paid deputy or curate). *Commenda* had long been used to supplement the income of students, professors, ecclesiastical diplomats, cardinals, and others. The appointment of cardinals or even laymen as abbots *in commendam* was a longstanding abuse that was not effectively dealt with until the Council of Trent.

45. A monk who had abandoned his monastery without permission was deemed "apostate." In Luther's day, such renegade monks, wandering about in their garb and exercising the rights and privileges of their order, were a common sight. They were a nuisance to the resident parish clergy and often disrupted parish life.

46. Offices that cannot be combined in the hands of one officeholder.

47. In this context, "gloss" means a specious, self-serving interpretation and application of a word or expression. Luther is not referring to the "ordinary glosses" (*glossa ordinaria*), which were the authoritative commentaries on canon law by medieval jurists (glossators).

48. The *datarius* was the head of the *Dataria apostolica*, the bureau of the

benefices like a bundle of sticks, and they are all regarded as one benefice. There is at present a certain papal courtier[t] in Rome who alone holds twenty-two parishes, seven priories, as well as forty-four benefices.[49] All these are held by the help of that masterly gloss, which declares that this is not against canon law. What the cardinals and other prelates get out of it is anybody's guess. And this is the way the Germans are to have their purses emptied and their insolence deflated.

Another of these glosses is the *administratio*. This means that a man may hold, in addition to his bishopric, some abbacy or dignity and all its emoluments, without having the title attached to it. He is simply called the "administrator."[50] At Rome it is sufficient to change a word or two but leave the actuality what it was before. It is as if I were to teach that we were now to call the brothel-keeper the mayor's wife. She still remains what she was before. This kind of Romish regime Peter foretold in 2 Pet. 2[:1, 3], "False teachers will come who will deal with you in greed and lying words for their gain."

Our worthy Roman Avarice has devised another technique. He sells and bestows benefices on the condition that the vendor or bestower retains reversionary rights to them. In that event, when the incumbent dies the benefices automatically revert to him who had sold, bestowed, or surrendered them in the first instance. In this way, they have made hereditary property out of the benefices. Nobody else can come into possession of them except the man to whom the seller is willing to dispose of them, or to whom he bequeaths his rights at death. Besides, there are many who transfer to another the mere title to a benefice, but from which the titleholder does not draw a cent. Today, too, it has become an established custom to confer a benefice on a man while reserving a portion of the annual income for oneself. This used to be called simony.[51] There are many more things of this sort than can be counted. They treat benefices more shamefully than the heathen soldiers treated Christ's clothes at the foot of the cross.

t   Luther's word is *kurtisan* (from the Latin *curtisanus*), the common (pejorative) term for a member of the papal Curia, or for a clergyman who secured his appointment from the Roman Curia.

papal Curia responsible for drafting, registering, and dating (hence the name) such written decisions of the pope as dispensations, appointments to benefices, and so forth. Fees were charged for its services.

49. The papal courtier referred to by Luther has not been identified. But there is documentation for two Germans, Johannes Zink (d. c. 1527) and Johannes Ingenwinkel (1469–1535), who accumulated papal appointments in Rome. In the period 1513 to 1521, Zink received fifty-six appointments; in the years 1496 to 1521 Ingenwinkel received 106. See Aloys Schulte, *Die Fugger in Rom 1495–1523*, vol. 1 (Leipzig: Verlag von Duncker, 1904), 282–306.

50. As, for example, in the case of Albrecht von Brandenburg, who was the administrator of Halberstadt; see above, n. 41.

51. Simony (named for Simon Magus; cf. Acts 8:18-20) was the buying or selling of an ecclesiastical office for money, favors, or any kind of material reward. It was strictly against canon law but widely practiced nonetheless.

52. From 1484 popes claimed and occasionally exercised the right to issue decrees, the content of which had been determined by the pope *motu proprio* ("of his own accord"), without consulting the cardinals or any other authorities, for reasons that he himself found sufficient.

But all that has been said up till now has been going on for so long that it has become established custom at Rome. Yet Avarice has come up with something else, which I hope may be his last and choke him. The pope has a noble little device called *pectoralis reservatio*, meaning mental reservation,ᵘ and *proprius motus*, meaning the arbitrary exercise of his authority.[52] It goes like this. A certain man goes to Rome and succeeds in procuring a benefice. It is duly signed and sealed in the customary manner. Then another candidate comes along, who brings money or else has rendered services to the pope, which bears no mention here, and desires the same benefice of the pope. The pope then gives it to him and takes it away from the other. If anybody complains that this is not right, then the Most Holy Father has to find some excuse lest he be accused of a flagrant violation of [canon] law. He then says that he had mentally reserved that particular benefice to himself and had retained full rights of disposal over it, although he had neither given it a thought in his whole life nor even heard of it. In this way, he has now found his usual little gloss. As pope he can tell lies, deceive, and make everybody look like a fool. And all this he does openly and unashamedly. And yet he still wants to be the head of Christendom, but lets himself be ruled by the evil spirit in obvious lies.

The pope's arbitrary and deceptive reservation now creates such a state of affairs in Rome that it defies description. There is buying, selling, bartering, exchanging, trading, pretense, deceit, robbery, theft, luxury, whoring, knavery, and every sort of contempt of God. Even the rule of the Antichrist could not be more scandalous. Venice, Antwerp, and Cairo[53] have nothing on this fair at Rome and all that goes on there. In these places there is still some regard for right and reason, but in Rome the devil himself is in charge. And out of this sea the same kind of morality flows into the whole world. Is it any wonder that people like this are terrified of reformation and of a free council, and prefer rather to set all the kings and princes at enmity lest in their unity they

53. Three major ports in the commerce of the day, famed as centers of vice.

u   Literally, "reservation in the breast or heart."

should call a council? Who could bear to have such villainy brought to light?

Finally, the pope has built his own emporium for all this noble commerce, that is, the house of the *datarius* in Rome.[v] All who deal in benefices and livings must go there. Here they have to buy their glosses, transact their business, and get authority to practice such arch-knavery. There was a time when Rome was still lenient. In those days, people just had to buy justice or suppress it with money. But Rome has become so expensive today that it allows no one to practice such knavery unless he has first bought the right to do so. If that is not a brothel above all imaginable brothels, then I do not know what brothels are.

If you have money in such an emporium, you can obtain all the things we have just discussed. Indeed, not just these! Here usury[54] becomes honest money; the possession of property acquired by theft or robbery is legalized. Here vows are dissolved; monks are granted freedom to leave their orders. Here marriage is on sale to the clergy. Here the children of whores can be legitimized. Here all dishonor and shame can be made to look like honor and glory. Here every kind of fault and blemish is knighted and ennobled. Here marriage within the forbidden degrees or otherwise forbidden is rendered acceptable. O what assessing and fleecing take place there! It seems as though canon law were instituted solely for the purpose of setting a great many money traps from which anyone who wants to be a Christian must purchase his freedom. In fact, here the devil becomes a saint, and a god as well. What cannot be done anywhere else in heaven or on earth, can be done in this emporium. They call these things *compositiones*! Compositions indeed! Better named confusions.[55] Compared with the exactions of this holy house the Rhine toll is a poor sum indeed.[56]

Let no one accuse me of exaggeration. It is all so open that even in Rome they have to admit that the state of affairs there is more atrocious than anyone can say. I have not yet stirred the real hellish dregs of their personal vices—nor do

54. Canon law still condemned as usury the charging by Christians of interest on loans to other Christians.

55. *Compositiones* were the fees paid for dispensations from the provisions of canon law. Luther makes a pun on *compositiones* (literally, "things in good order") and *confusiones* ("things in disorder").

56. Princes and nobles who had fortresses along the Rhine commonly exacted tolls from passing merchant ships.

v   See n. 48 above.

57. The Fugger firm of Augsburg was the greatest international banking house of the sixteenth century. It numbered popes, bishops, emperors, kings, and princes among its clients and benefactors. The Fuggers advanced to Charles V the funds needed to secure his election as emperor. Similarly, they advanced to Albrecht von Brandenburg the monies required for the purchase from Rome of the dispensations he needed to become archbishop of Mainz (see p. 399, n. 41).

58. A bull is a solemn mandate of the pope on any subject under his authority (the definition of doctrine, the granting of privileges, etc.). The name "bull" derives from the Latin *bulla*, a term for the seal attached to an official document.

59. Certificates that entitled the bearer to choose his or her own confessor and authorized the confessor to confer absolution for offenses normally reserved to the jurisdiction of bishops or the pope.

60. *Butterbriefe* was the popular term for written dispensations to consume butter, cheese, and milk during Lent.

61. The Campo de' Fiore was a Roman marketplace that Pope Eugene IV and his successors restored and developed at great expense. The Belvedere, originally a garden house in the Vatican, was turned into an elegant banquet hall and then used by Pope Julius II to store his collection of ancient art (e.g., the Apollo Belvedere). Luther hints that indulgence money was lavished on such projects rather than used for constructing St. Peter's in Rome as advertised.

I want to. I speak only of ordinary, well-known matters, and still cannot find adequate words for them. Bishops, priests, and above all the theologians in the universities ought to have done their duty and with common accord written against such goings-on and cried out against them. This is what they are paid to do! But the truth is found on the other side of the page.[w]

I must take leave of this subject with one final word. Since this Boundless Avarice is not satisfied with all this wealth, wealth with which three great kings would be content, he now begins to transfer this trade and sell it to the Fuggers of Augsburg.[57] The lending, trading, and buying of bishoprics and benefices, and the commerce in ecclesiastical holdings, have now come to the right place. Now spiritual and secular goods have become one. I would now like to hear of somebody clever enough to imagine what Roman Avarice could do more than what it has already done, unless perhaps Fugger were to transfer or sell this present combination of two lines of business to somebody else. I really think it has just reached the limit.

As for what they have stolen in all lands, and still steal and extort, through indulgences, bulls,[58] confessional letters,[59] butter letters,[60] and other *confessionalia*—all this is just patchwork. It is just as if one were rolled dice with a devil right into hell. Not that these things bring in little money—for a powerful king could well support himself on such proceeds—but it is not to be compared with the streams of treasure referred to above. I shall say nothing at present about where this indulgence money has gone. I shall have more to say about that later. The Campo de' Fiore and the Belvedere and certain other places probably know something about that.[61]

Since, then, such devilish rule is not only barefaced robbery, deceit, and the tyranny of the gates of hell but also ruinous to the body and soul of Christendom, it is our duty to exercise all diligence to protect Christendom from

w   I.e., the opposite is the case.

such misery and destruction. If we want to fight against the Turks, let us begin here where they are worst of all. If we are right in hanging thieves and beheading robbers, why should we let Roman Avarice go free? He is the worst thief and robber that has ever been or could ever come into the world, and all in the holy name of Christ and St. Peter! Who can put up with it a moment longer and say nothing? Almost everything Avarice possesses has been procured by theft and robbery. It has never been otherwise, as all the history books prove. The pope never purchased such extensive holdings that the income from his *officia*ˣ should amount to one million ducats, over and above the gold mines we have just been discussing and the income from his lands. Nor did Christ and St. Peter bequeath it to him. Neither has anyone given or lent it to him. Neither is it his by virtue of ancient rights or usage. Tell me, then, from what source could he have obtained it? Learn a lesson from this, and watch carefully what they are after and what they say when they send out their legates to collect money to fight the Turks.

Now, although I am too insignificant a man to make concrete proposals for the improvement of this dreadful state of affairs, nevertheless I shall sing my fool's song through to the end and say, so far as I am able, what could and should be done, either by secular authority or by a general council.

1. Every prince, every noble, every city should henceforth forbid their subjects to pay annates to Rome and should abolish them entirely. The pope has broken the agreement and made the annates a robbery to the injury and shame of the whole German nation. He gives them to his friends, sells them for huge sums of money, and uses them to endow offices. In so doing he has lost his right to them and deserves punishment. Consequently, secular authority is under obligation to protect the innocent and prevent injustice, as Paul teaches in Romans 13, and St. Peter in 1 Pet. 2[:14], and even the canon law in Case 16, Question 7, [canon 31], *de filiis*.[62] From this came the basis for saying to the pope and his own

62. The correct name of the canon is *Filiis vel nepotibus*; Friedberg 1:809. It provides that when the endowment provided for a church is misused, and appeals to the bishop and archbishop fail to correct the abuse, the heirs of the person who established the endowment may appeal to the secular courts. Luther wants this principle applied to annates as well.

x   The curial offices that could be purchased; see p. 396, n. 36.

63. Although Luther here adheres to the traditional threefold division of society into priests, rulers, and workers (or farmers), he does so in accordance with the position taken in his assault on the first wall (pp. 381–85), namely that secular rulers have the obligation to protect their subjects against secular crimes committed by the clergy.

[the clergy], "*Tu ora*, thou shalt pray"; to the emperor and his servants, "*Tu protege*, thou shalt protect"; to the common man, "*Tu labora*, thou shalt labor," not, however, as though each person were not to pray, protect, and labor. (For the one who performs any task diligently does nothing but pray, protect, and labor.) But to each a special work is assigned.[63]

2. Since the pope with his Romish tricks—his *commenda*, coadjutors, reservations, *gratiae expectativae*, papal months, incorporations, unions, pensions, *pallia*, chancery rules, and such knavery[y]—usurps for himself all the German foundations without authority and right and gives and sells them to foreigners at Rome who do nothing for Germany in return, and since he robs the local bishops of their rights and makes mere ciphers and dummies of them, and thereby acts contrary to his own canon law, common sense, and reason, it has finally reached the point where the livings and benefices are, out of sheer greed, sold to coarse, unlettered donkeys and ignorant knaves at Rome. Pious and learned people do not benefit from their service or skill. Consequently the poor German people must go without competent and learned prelates and be destroyed.

For this reason, the Christian nobility should set itself against the pope as against a common enemy and destroyer of Christendom for the salvation of the poor souls who perish because of this tyranny. The Christian nobility should ordain, order, and decree that henceforth no further benefice shall be drawn into the hands of Rome, and that hereafter no appointment shall be obtained there in any manner whatsoever, but that the benefices should be dragged from this tyrannical authority and kept out of his reach. The nobility should restore to the local bishops their right and responsibility to administer the benefices in the German nation to the best of their ability. And when a papal courtier comes along,[z] he should be given a strict order to keep out, to jump into the Rhine or the nearest river, and give the

y With the exception of *gratiae expectivae* (promises to bestow a benefice not yet vacant), these "tricks" were explained earlier; see above, pp. 401–5, with the explanatory notes.

z Cf. p. 403, n. 49 and note *t*.

Romish ban with all its seals and letters a nice, cold bath. If this happened, they would sit up and take notice in Rome. They would not think that the Germans are always dull and drunk but have really become Christian again. They would realize that the Germans do not intend to permit the holy name of Christ, in whose name all this knavery and destruction of souls goes on, to be scoffed at and scorned any longer, and that they have more regard for God's honor than for the authority of mortals.

3. An imperial law should be issued that no bishop's cloak [*pallium*] and no confirmation of any dignity whatsoever shall henceforth be secured from Rome, but that the ordinance of the most holy and famous Council of Nicaea be restored. This ordinance decreed that a bishop shall be confirmed by the two nearest bishops or by the archbishop.[64] If the pope breaks the statutes of this and of all other councils, what is the use of holding councils? Who has given him the authority to despise the decisions of councils and tear them to shreds like this? Perhaps we should depose all bishops, archbishops, and primates[65] and make ordinary pastors of them, with only the pope as their superior, as he now is. The pope allows no proper authority or responsibility to the bishops, archbishops, and primates. He usurps everything for himself and lets them keep only the name and the empty title. It has even gone so far that by papal exemption the monasteries, abbots, and prelates as well are removed from the regular authority of the bishops.[66] Consequently there is no longer any order in Christendom. The inevitable result of all this is what has happened already: relaxation of punishment and the license to do evil all over the world. I certainly fear that the pope may properly be called "the man of sin" [2 Thess. 2:3]. Who but the pope can be blamed for there being no discipline, no punishment, no government, no order in Christendom? By his usurpation of power he ties the prelates' hands and takes away their rod of discipline. He opens his hands to all those set under him, and gives away or sells them freedom.[a]

64. Canon 4 of the Council of Nicaea (325). Here Luther still assumes that the existing ecclesiastical hierarchy would be preserved and reformed.

65. A primate was the highest-ranking archbishop of a country; in the Empire it was the archbishop of Mainz.

66. It was common practice for monastic houses to be removed from the jurisdiction of the local bishop and placed directly under that of the pope. Indeed, it was all but universal in the case of the houses of the mendicant orders.

a I.e., freedom from the jurisdiction of the local prelate.

67. This was actually a decree of the Council of Sardica (343), but it was incorporated into canon law with inaccurate attribution to the Council of Nicaea; see Friedberg 1:520.

68. The councils of Constance and Basel had both tried to put an end to the evocation of secular cases to the Roman Curia, but it remained one of the most often-repeated of the grievances of the Holy Roman Empire against Rome. See Benrath, 97–98, n. 43; RTA 2:672, par. 1.

Lest the pope complain that he is being robbed of his authority, it should be decreed that in those cases where the primates or the archbishops are unable to settle a case, or when a dispute arises between them, then the matter should be laid before the pope, but not every little thing. It was done this way in former times, and this was the way the famous Council of Nicaea decreed.[67] Whatever can be settled without the pope, then, should be settled in such a way that his holiness is not burdened with such minor matters, but gives himself to prayer, study and the care of all Christendom. This is what he claims to do. This is what the apostles did. They said in Acts 6[:2-4], "It is not right that we should leave the Word of God and serve tables, but we will hold to preaching and prayer, and set others over that work." But now Rome stands for nothing else than the despising of the gospel and prayer, and for the serving of tables, that is, temporal things. The government of the apostles and of the pope have as much in common as Christ has with Lucifer, heaven with hell, night with day. Yet the pope is called "Vicar of Christ" and "Successor to the Apostles."

4. It should be decreed that no secular matter is to be referred to Rome, but that all such cases shall be left to secular authority, as the Romanists themselves prescribe in that canon law of theirs, which they do not observe.[68] It should be the pope's duty to be the most learned in the Scriptures and the holiest (not in name only but in fact) and to regulate matters that concern the faith and holy life of Christians. He should hold the primates and archbishops to this task, and help them in dealing with these matters and taking care of these responsibilities. This is what St. Paul teaches in 1 Cor. 6[:7], and he takes the Corinthians severely to task for their concern with worldly things. That such matters are dealt with in Rome causes unbearable grief in every land. It increases the costs, and, moreover, these judges do not know the usage, laws, and customs of these lands, so that they often do violence to the facts and base their decisions on their own laws and precedents. As a result, the contesting parties often suffer injustice.

Moreover, the horrible fleecing practiced by the officials[69] must be forbidden in every diocese, so that they no longer assume jurisdiction over anything except matters of faith and morals and leave matters of money and property, life and honor, to the secular judges. Secular judges, therefore, should not allow sentences of excommunication and banishment in cases where faith and morals are not involved. Spiritual authority should rule over matters that are spiritual, as reason teaches. Spiritual goods, however, do not consist of money or material things but rather of faith and good works.

One might, nonetheless, grant that cases concerning benefices or livings be tried before bishops, archbishops and primates. Accordingly, whenever disputes or conflicts needed to be resolved, the primate of Germany could hold a general consistory with its jurists and judges, which would have the same authority as that of the *signatura gratiae* and *signatura justitiae* in Rome.[70] Cases in Germany would, by means of appeal, be brought before it and transacted in good order. One could not be required to pay for this by occasional presents and gifts, as is the case at Rome, as a result of which they have grown accustomed to the selling of justice and injustice. This is because the pope does not pay them a salary, but lets them grow fat from gifts. For no one at Rome cares anything about what is right or wrong, only about what is money and what is not. One might, rather, pay for this [court] from the annates, or in some other way devised by those who are better informed and more experienced in these things than I am. All I seek to do is to arouse and set to thinking those who have the ability and inclination to help the German nation be free and Christian again after the wretched, heathenish, and un-Christian reign of the pope.

5. Reservations should no longer be valid,[b] and no more benefices should be seized by Rome, even if the incumbent dies or there is a dispute, or even if the incumbent is a member of the pope's household or on the staff of a cardinal. And it must be strictly forbidden and prevented for any

69. The *officialis* was the presiding judge of a bishop's court.

70. The supreme tribunal of the church was the *Signatura*, which was divided into the *Signatura gratiae*, presided over by the pope himself, and the *Signatura justitiae*, headed by a cardinal. The latter resolved conflicts of jurisdiction among various legal entities in the Curia. The former handled the pope's responses to requests for privileges or favors and in so doing could grant exemptions from church law. The proposal to turn the honorary primacy of the archbishop of Mainz into the effective headship of a German church with extensive administrative independence of Rome was first advanced by the Alsatian humanist Jakob Wimpfeling (1450–1528) in a memorandum submitted to Emperor Maximilian I in 1510. A shortened version of the memorandum had been published in May 1520, but Luther appears to have had access to the full manuscript. See Benrath, 98, n. 45.

b See p. 398, n. 38.

papal courtier*[c]* to contest any benefice whatsoever, to summon pious priests to court, harass them, or force them into lawsuits. If, in consequence of this prohibition, any ban or ecclesiastical pressure should come from Rome, it should be disregarded, just as though a thief were to put a man under the ban because he would not let him steal. Indeed, they should be severely punished for blasphemous misuse of the ban and the divine name to strengthen their hand at robbery, and for desiring, by means of lies and fabrications, to compel us to endure and praise such blasphemy of God's name and such abuse of Christian authority, and to be participants in their rascality in the sight of God. We are responsible before God to oppose them, as St. Paul in Rom. 1[:32] reproves as worthy of death not only those who do such things, but also those who approve and permit them to be done. Most unbearable of all is the lying *reservatio pectoralis,*[d] whereby Christendom is so scandalously and openly put to shame and scorn because its head deals with open lies and for filthy lucre unashamedly deceives and fools everybody.

6. The *casus reservati,* reserved cases,[71] should also be abolished. They are not only the means of extorting much money from the people, but by means of them the ruthless tyrants ensnare and confuse many tender consciences, intolerably injuring their faith in God. This is especially true of the ridiculous, childish cases they make such a fuss about in the bull *Coena Domini,*[72] sins which should not even be called everyday sins, much less so great that the pope cannot remit them by indulgence. Examples of these sins are hindering a pilgrim on his way to Rome, supplying weapons to the Turk, or counterfeiting papal briefs.[73] They make fools of us with such crude, silly, clumsy goings-on! Sodom and Gomorrah, and all the sins that are or may be committed against the commandments of God, are not reserved cases. But what God has never commanded and they themselves have imagined—these must be reserved cases, in order that no one be prevented from bringing money to Rome, so that

71. Those cases in which the granting of absolution was reserved to the pope.

72. Since the fourteenth century it had been the custom to publish at Rome on Maundy Thursday an updated version of the bull *In coena Domini,* a catalog of heresies and offenses punishable by excommunication, absolution for which was reserved to the pope. After his excommunication in 1521, Luther's name was added to the list of heretics.

73. A decree in the form of a letter emanating from the pope, simpler in form than a bull but of comparable authority.

c   See p. 403, n. 49.

d   I.e., mental reservation; see above, p. 404.

they may live in the lap of luxury, safe from the Turks and by their wanton, worthless bulls and briefs keep the world subjected to their tyranny.

Such knowledge should properly be available from all priests or be a public ordinance, namely, that no secret, undenounced sin constitutes a reserved case; and that every priest has the power to remit every sin no matter what it is.[e] Where sins are secret, neither abbot, bishop, nor pope has the power to reserve one of them to himself. If they did that, their action would be null and void. They ought even to be punished as people who without any right at all presume to make judgments in God's stead, and thereby ensnare and burden poor and ignorant consciences. In those cases, however, where open and notorious sins are committed, especially sins against God's commandments, then there are indeed grounds for reserved cases. But even then there should not be too many of them, and they should not be reserved arbitrarily and without cause. For Christ did not set tyrants in his church, but shepherds, as Peter said in the last chapter of his first epistle [1 Pet. 5:2-3].

7. The Roman See should do away with the *officia*[f] and cut down the creeping, crawling swarm of vermin at Rome, so that the pope's household can be supported out of the pope's own pocket. The pope should not allow his court to surpass the courts of all kings in pomp and extravagance, because this kind of thing not only has never been of any use to the cause of the Christian faith but also has kept the courtiers from study and prayer until they are hardly able to speak about the faith at all. This they proved quite flagrantly at this last Roman council,[74] in which, among many other childish and frivolous things, they decreed that the human soul is immortal and that every priest must say his

74. The Fifth Lateran Council (1412–1417), convened by Julius II.

e   Thesis 6 (*95 Theses*, above, p. 35) stated, "The pope cannot remit any guilt except by declaring and confirming its remission by God or, of course, by remitting guilt in [legal] cases reserved to himself." In terms of divine grace and the removal of guilt, priests simply announced God's forgiveness. Regarding especially heinous sins, ecclesiastical absolution was restricted to the papal see.

f   See p. 396, n. 36.

prayers once a month unless he wants to lose his benefice. How can the affairs of Christendom and matters of faith be settled by people who are hardened and blinded by gross avarice, wealth, and worldly splendor, and who now for the first time decree that the soul is immortal? It is no small shame to the whole of Christendom that they deal so disgracefully with the faith at Rome. If they had less wealth and pomp, they could pray better and study to be worthy and diligent in dealing with matters of faith, as was the case in former times, when bishops did not presume to be the kings of all kings.

8. The harsh and terrible oaths that the bishops are wrongfully compelled to swear to the pope should be abolished. These oaths bind the bishops like servants and are decreed in that arbitrary, stupid, worthless, and unlearned chapter, *Significasti*.[75] Is it not enough that they burden us in body, soul, and property with their countless foolish laws by which they weaken faith and waste Christendom, without also making a prisoner of the bishop both as a person as well as in his office and function? In addition, they have also assumed the investiture,[76] which in ancient times was the right of the German emperor, and in France and other countries investiture still belongs to the king. They had great wars and disputes with the emperors about this matter until finally they had the brazen effrontery to take it over, and have held it until now; just as though the Germans more than all other Christians on earth had to be the silly fools of the pope and the Romanist See and do and put up with what no one else will either put up with or do. Since this is sheer robbery and violence, hinders the regular authority of the bishop, and injures poor souls, the emperor and his nobles are duty-bound to prevent and punish such tyranny.

9. The pope should have no authority over the emperor, except the right to anoint and crown him at the altar, just as a bishop crowns a king. We should never again yield to that devilish pride which requires the emperor to kiss the pope's feet, or sit at his feet, or, as they say, hold his stirrup or the bridle of his mule when he mounts to go riding. Still less should he do homage and swear faithful allegiance to

75. It provided that no pallium (above, p. 400, n. 42) was to be bestowed on an archbishop until he had sworn an oath of allegiance to the Holy See; Friedberg 2:49–50.

76. Investiture was the ceremony of installing a bishop in office by bestowing on him the staff and ring that were the symbols of his authority. In Germany this was a matter complicated by the fact that most bishops were the secular rulers of an imperial territory (e.g., the electorate of Mainz) as well as the overseers of an ecclesiastical benefice (e.g., the archbishopric of Mainz). In the eleventh and twelfth centuries, this situation had produced a bitter struggle between pope and emperor over who controlled the investiture of bishops. The Concordat of Worms (1122) took away from the emperor the right to invest bishops with ring and staff and left him with only the right to invest them with authority as secular rulers.

the pope, as the popes brazenly demand as though they had a right to it. The chapter *Solite*,[g] which sets papal authority above imperial authority, is not worth a cent, and the same goes for all those who base their authority on it or pay any deference to it. For it does nothing else than force the holy words of God, and wrest them out of their true meaning to conform to their own fond imaginations, as I have shown in a Latin treatise.[h]

This most extreme, arrogant, and wanton presumption of the pope has been devised by the devil, who under cover of this intends to usher in the Antichrist and raise the pope above God, as many are now doing and even have already done. It is not proper for the pope to exalt himself above the secular authorities, except in spiritual offices such as preaching and giving absolution. In other matters, the pope is subject to the crown, as Paul and Peter teach in Rom. 13[:1-7] and 1 Pet. 2[:13], and as I have explained above.[i]

The pope is not a vicar of Christ in heaven but only of Christ as he walked the earth. Christ in heaven, in the form of a ruler, needs no vicar, but sits on his throne and sees everything, does everything, knows everything, and has all power. But Christ needs a vicar in the form of a servant, the form in which he went about on earth, working, preaching, suffering, and dying. Now the Romanists turn all that upside down. They take the heavenly and kingly form from Christ and give it to the pope, and leave the form of a servant to perish completely. He might almost be the Counter-Christ, whom the Scriptures call Antichrist,[j] for all his nature, work, and pretensions run counter to Christ and only blot out Christ's nature and destroy his work.

It is also ridiculous and childish for the pope, on the basis of such perverted and deluded reasoning, to claim in his decretal *Pastoralis* that he is rightful heir to the emperorship

---

g   Friedberg 2:196.

h   *Resolutio Lutheriana super propositione XIII de potestate papae* (1519) in WA 2:217–21, 8, part of the Leipzig Debate with Johann Eck in 1519.

i   See pp. 364–85.

j   See p. 387, n. 24.

in the event of a vacancy.*k* Who has given him this right? Was it Christ when he said, "The princes of the Gentiles are lords, but it shall not be so among you" [Luke 22:25-26]? Or did Peter bequeath it to him? It makes me angry that we have to read and learn such shameless, gross, and idiotic lies in canon law and must even hold them as Christian doctrine when they are devilish lies.

That impossible lie, the *Donation of Constantine*,[77] is the same sort of thing. It must have been some special plague from God that so many intelligent people have let themselves be talked into accepting such lies. They are so crude and clumsy that I should imagine any drunken peasant could lie more adroitly and skillfully. How can a person rule and at the same time preach, pray, study, and care for the poor? Yet these are the duties which most properly and peculiarly belong to the pope, and they were so earnestly imposed by Christ that he even forbade his disciples to take cloak or money with them [Matt. 10:9-10]. Christ commanded this because it is almost impossible for anybody to fulfill these duties if they have to look after one single household. Yet the pope would rule an empire and still remain pope. This is what those rogues have thought up, who under the cover of the pope's name would like to be lords of the world and would gladly restore the Roman Empire to its former state through the pope and in the name of Christ.

10. The pope should restrain himself, take his fingers out of the pie, and claim no title to the kingdom of Naples and Sicily.[78] He has exactly as much right to that kingdom as I have, and yet he wants to be its overlord. It is property gotten by robbery and violence, like almost all his other possessions. The emperor, therefore, should not grant him this realm, and where it has been granted, he should no longer give his consent.[79] Instead, he should draw the pope's attention to the Bible and the prayer book, that he preach and pray and leave the government of lands and people—especially those that no one has given to him—to the lords.

77. This document, the *Donation of Constantine* (Mirbt-Aland, no. 504), purported to be the testament of Emperor Constantine. It conferred on the pope temporal sovereignty in Rome, Italy, and "all the western regions" and was used to bolster not only papal claims to secular rule in Italy but also the claim that the secular authority of kings and emperors was a gracious concession from the pope, in whom supreme secular and ecclesiastical authority were united. In 1440 the Italian humanist Lorenzo Valla (c. 1407–1457) demonstrated that the *Donation* was a forgery. Shortly before writing this treatise, Luther had read the edition of Valla's treatise published by Ulrich von Hutten in 1517. For an abbreviated English version, see Henry Bettenson and Chris Maunder, eds., *Documents of the Christian Church*, 4th ed. (New York: Oxford University Press, 2011), 102–6.

78. Since 1060, popes had claimed feudal sovereignty over the kingdom of Naples and Sicily, where much land had been given to the church since late antiquity. These claims, justified on the basis of the *Donation of Constantine* (see preceding note), were hotly contested.

79. At this time the kingdom was contested between the royal houses of France and Spain. Emperor Charles V was also King Charles I of Spain.

---

k   *Clem.* lib 2, tit. 11. cap. 2 (Friedberg 2:1151–53).

The same goes for Bologna, Imola, Vicenza, Ravenna, and all the territories in the March of Ancona, Romagna, and other lands that the pope has seized by force and possesses without right.[80] Moreover, the pope has meddled in these things against every express command of Christ and St. Paul. For as St. Paul says, "No one should be entangled in worldly affairs who should tend to being a soldier of God."[l] Now the pope should be the head and chief of these soldiers, and yet he meddles in worldly affairs more than any emperor or king. We have to pull him out of these affairs and let him tend to being a soldier. Even Christ, whose vicar the pope boasts he is, was never willing to have anything to do with secular rule. In fact, when somebody sought a judgment from him in the matter of a brother's action, he said to that man, "Who made me a judge over you?" [Luke 12:14]. But the pope rushes in without invitation and boldly takes hold of everything as if he were a god, until he no longer knows who Christ is, whose vicar he pretends to be.

11. Further, the kissing of the pope's feet should cease.[m] It is an un-Christian, indeed, an anti-Christian thing for a poor sinful man to let his feet be kissed by one who is a hundred times better than himself. If it is done in honor of his authority, why does the pope not do the same to others in honor of their holiness? Compare them with each other— Christ and the pope. Christ washed his disciples' feet and dried them, but the disciples never washed his feet [John 13:4-16]. The pope, as though he were higher than Christ, turns that about and allows his feet to be kissed as a great favor. Though properly, if anyone wanted to do so, the pope ought to use all his power to prevent it, as did St. Paul and Barnabas, who would not let the people of Lystra pay them divine honor, but said, "We are mortals like you" [Acts 14:15]. But our flatterers have gone so far as to make an idol [of the pope] for us, so that no one fears or honors God as

80. All these were components of the states of the church, the conglomeration of territories in central Italy over which the pope exercised direct secular rule. It was in large measure the result of claims to secular authority in Italy that the papacy was inextricably involved in the political and military struggles of Italy and western Europe.

l This is a free rendering of the Vulgate text of 2 Tim. 2:4.

m See above, p. 414 and below, n. 81., p. 418.

81. Both kissing the pope's feet and his being carried were depicted in *Passional Christi und Antichristi* (1521; WA 9:677–715 with the appendix), with woodcuts by Lukas Cranach Sr. (1472–1553) and comments by Philip Melanchthon and Martin Luther contrasting papal practices with Christ's passion. For depiction of this, see below, p. 523.

The pope being carried in a procession.

much as he fears and honors the pope. They will stand for that, but not for diminishing the pope's majesty by so much as a hairsbreadth. If they were only Christian and esteemed God's honor more than their own, the pope would never be happy to see God's honor despised and his own exalted. Nor would he let anyone honor him until he saw that God's honor was once more exalted and raised higher than his own.[81, n]

Another example of the same scandalous pride is that the pope is not satisfied to ride or be driven, but, although strong and in good health, has himself borne by men like an idol and with unheard-of splendor. Dear readers, how does such satanic pride compare with Christ, who went on foot, as did all his disciples? Where has there ever been a worldly monarch who went about in such worldly pomp and glory as he who wants to be the head of all those who ought to despise and flee from the pomp and vanity of this world, that is, the Christians? Not that we should bother ourselves very much about him as a person, but we certainly ought to fear the wrath of God if we flatter this sort of pride and do not show our indignation. It is enough that the pope rants and plays the fool in this way. But it is too much if we approve of it and grant it to him.

What Christian heart can or should take pleasure in seeing that when the pope wishes to receive communion, he sits quietly like a gracious lord and has the sacrament brought to him on a golden rod by a bowing cardinal on bended knee? As though the holy sacrament were not worthy that the pope, a poor, stinking sinner, should rise and show respect to his God, when all other Christians, who are much holier than the Most Holy Father the pope, receive it with all due reverence! Would it be a wonder if God sent down a plague upon us all

n   The remainder of this section was not included in the first printing of the treatise. Along with two other passages indicated in the

because we tolerate and praise such dishonor of God by our prelates, and make ourselves participants in this damnable pride by our silence or flattery?

It is the same when the pope carries the sacrament in procession. He must be carried, but the sacrament is set before him like a jug of wine on a table. At Rome Christ counts for nothing, but the pope counts for everything. And yet the Romanists want to compel us—and even use threats—to approve, praise, and honor these sins of the Antichrist, even though they are against God and all Christian doctrine. Help us, O God, to get a free, general council, which will teach the pope that he, too, is a mortal and not more than God, as he presumes himself to be!

12. Pilgrimages to Rome should either be abolished or else no one should be allowed to make such a pilgrimage simply out of curiosity or pious devotion, unless his parish priest, his town authorities, or his overlord confirm that he has a good and sufficient reason for doing so.[82] I say this not because pilgrimages are bad, but because they are ill advised at this time. For at Rome they do not see a good example, but rather pure scandal. The Romanists themselves devised the saying, "The nearer Rome, the worse the Christians."[o] They bring back [from Rome] contempt for God and his commandments. They say the first time a man goes to Rome he seeks a rascal; the second time he finds one; the third time he brings him back home with him.[p] Now, however, they have become so accomplished that they can make three pilgrimages in one and have truly brought back to us from Rome such things that it would be better never to have seen Rome or known anything about it.

Even if this were not the case, there is still another and a better reason: simple people are led into a false estimation

82. Although there were many other popular destinations for pilgrims, like Jerusalem or Santiago de Compostela, Rome with its holy places was by far the favorite.

notes below, it was inserted into the second printing, published at Wittenberg in November 1520.

o   A common proverb in German and Latin; see Wander, 3:1714, no. 21f.

p   Wander, 3:1717–18, no. 72. See the remark of Ulrich von Hutten in his *Vadiscus*: "Three things there are which those who go to Rome usually bring back with them: a bad conscience, a ruined stomach, and an empty purse." See *Ulrich von Hutten Schriften*, ed. Eduard Böcking, vol. 4: *Gespräche* (Leipzig, 1860), 169.

and misconception about the divine commandments. For they think that going on a pilgrimage is a precious good work, which is not true. It is scarcely a good work—frequently a wickedly deceptive work, for God has not commanded it. But God has commanded that a man should care for his wife and children, perform the duties of a husband, and serve and help his neighbor. Today it happens that a man makes a pilgrimage to Rome, spends fifty, maybe a hundred, gulden, something that nobody commanded him to do, and leaves his wife and child, or his neighbor at any rate, to suffer want back home. And yet the silly fool thinks he can gloss over such disobedience and contempt of the divine commandment with his self-assigned pilgrimage, which is really nothing but impertinence or a delusion of the devil. By encouraging this with their false, feigned, foolish "golden years,"[83] by which the people are excited, torn away from God's commandments and drawn to the seductive papal enterprise, the popes have done the very thing they ought to have prevented. But it has brought in money and fortified their counterfeit authority. That is why it had to go on, even though it is contrary to God or the salvation of souls.

To eradicate such false, seductive faith from the minds of simple Christian people, and to restore a right understanding of good works, all pilgrimages should be abolished. For there is no good in them, no commandment and no duty, but only countless occasions for sin and disdain of God's commandments. This is why there are so many beggars who commit all kinds of mischief by going on these pilgrimages, and who learn to beg when there is no need and become accustomed to it. This accounts for vagabondage and many ills about which I shall not speak here.

Whoever wants to go on a pilgrimage today or vow to make a pilgrimage should first explain the reasons for doing so to his priest or his lord. If it turns out that he wants to do it for the sake of a good work, then let the priest or lord put his foot down firmly and put an end to the vow and the good work as a devilish delusion. Let priest and lord show him how to use the money and effort [to be expended] on the pilgrimage for God's commandments and for works a

83. "Golden" or "jubilee" years were established by Pope Boniface VIII (c. 1235–1303) in 1300. Initially, every hundredth year was to be a jubilee, but by mid-fourteenth century it had become every fifty years, and by Luther's time it was every twenty-five years. During jubilee years, plenary indulgences were offered to pilgrims to Rome who visited the churches of the apostles a specified number of times. The pope received a handsome share of the pilgrims' free offerings, and the local economy benefited from their presence. Luther was doubtless aware that a large number of Germans went on pilgrimage to Rome in 1500.

thousand times better by spending it on his own family or on his poor neighbors. If, however, he wishes to make the pilgrimage out of curiosity, to see other lands and cities, he may be allowed to do so. But if he made the vow during an illness, then that vow must be annulled and canceled. God's commandment should be emphasized, so that henceforth he will be content to keep the vow made in baptism as well as the commandments of God.[q] Nevertheless, he may be allowed to perform his foolish vow just once to quiet his conscience. Nobody wants to walk in the straight path of God's commandments common to all of us. Everybody invents new ways and vows for himself as if he had already fulfilled all of God's commandments.

[13.] Next we come to the great crowd of those who make many vows but keep few. Do not be angry, my noble lords! I really mean it for the best. It is the bittersweet truth that the further building of mendicant cloisters[84] should not be permitted. God help us, there are already too many of them. Would God they were all dissolved, or at least combined into two or three orders! Their wandering around the country-side [begging] has never done any good and never will do any good. My advice is to join together ten of these houses or as many as need be, and make them a single institution for which adequate provision is made so that begging will not be necessary. It is far more important to consider what the common people need for their salvation than what St. Francis, St. Dominic, and St. Augustine,[85] or anyone else has established as a rule, especially because things have not turned out as they planned.

The mendicants should also be relieved of preaching and hearing confession, unless they are called to do this by the bishops, parishes, congregations, or the civil authorities. Nothing but hatred and envy between priests and monks has come out of this kind of preaching and confessing, and this has become a source of great offense and hindrance to the common people. It ought to stop because it can well

84. In contrast to monks, who lived by the Benedictine rule (cf. n. 94), mendicant friars (see the following note) sustained themselves in part by begging. Many cities had designated areas where this begging was permitted.

85. Luther is referring to the three principal mendicant orders, the Franciscans (founded by Francis of Assisi [c. 1181–1226]), the Dominicans (founded by Dominic [1170–1221]), and the Augustinian Hermits (his own order, which supposedly used a rule written by Augustine, bishop of Hippo).

---

q In *The Babylonian Captivity* of 1520 and in Martin Luther's *Judgment against Monastic Vows* of 1521, Luther will again emphasize baptismal vows. See above, p. 220.

St AVGVSTINE the Learned and painfull Bishop of Hippo, in Africa, for the space of 40 yeares where he dyed, in the 70th yeare of His Age, about ẏ yeare of or Lord 430. W. Marshall sculp.

Engraving of St. Augustine, bishop of Hippo, by William Marshall (d. 1649).

86. This applies particularly to the Franciscans and Augustinians. By the fifteenth century, both orders were divided between the Observants, who favored strict adherence to their order's rule, and the Conventuals, who took a more flexible view. Johann von Staupitz (c. 1460–1524), the head of the Augustinian order in Germany and Luther's own confessor, tried to unite the two groups. Luther's journey to Rome in 1511 was part of the legal conflict that this attempt produced.

be dispensed with. It looks suspiciously as though the Holy Roman See has purposely increased this army lest the priests and bishops, unable to stand the pope's tyranny any longer, some day become too powerful for him and start a reformation. That would be unbearable to his holiness.

At the same time, the manifold divisions and differences within one and the same order should be abolished. These divisions have arisen from time to time for very trivial reasons; they have been maintained for even more trivial reasons, and they quarrel with each other with unspeakable hatred and envy.[86] Nevertheless, the Christian faith, which can well exist without any of these distinctions, comes to grief because of both parties, and a good Christian life is valued and sought after only according to the standards of outward laws, works, and methods. Nothing comes of this but hypocrisy and the ruination of souls, as all can plainly see.

The pope must also be forbidden to found or approve any more of these orders; in fact, he must be ordered to abolish some and reduce the numbers of others. Inasmuch as faith in Christ, which alone is our chief possession and exists without any kind of orders, suffers no little danger in that people, confronted with so many and varied works and ways, will be easily led astray to live according to such works and ways rather than to pay heed to faith. And unless there are wise prelates in the monasteries who preach and stress faith more than the rule of the order, it is impossible for that order not to harm and mislead the simple souls who have regard only for works.

But in our day the prelates who did have faith and who founded the orders have passed away almost everywhere. It is just as it was centuries ago among the children of Israel. When the fathers who had known the wonders and the works of God had passed on, their children, ignorant of

God's works and of faith, immediately elevated idolatry and their own human works.ʳ In our day, unfortunately, these orders have no understanding of God's works or of faith, but make wretched martyrs of themselves by striving and working to keep their own rules, laws, and ways of life. Yet they never come to a right understanding of a spiritually good life. It is just as 2 Tim. 3[:5, 7] declares, "They have the appearance of a spiritual life, but there is nothing behind it: they are constantly learning, but they never come to a knowledge of what true spiritual life is." If the ruling prelate has no understanding of Christian faith, it would be better to have no monastery at all; for such a superior cannot govern an order without causing damage and destruction, and the holier and better the prelate appears to be in his external works, the more this is the case.

To my way of thinking, it would be a necessary measure, especially in our perilous times, to regulate convents and monasteries in the same way that they were regulated in the beginning, in the days of the apostles and for a long time afterward. In those days, convents and monasteries were all open for everyone to stay in them as long as they pleased. What else were the convents and monasteries but Christian schools where Scripture and the Christian life were taught, and where people were trained to rule and to preach?[87] Thus we read that St. Agnes went to school,[88] and we still see the same practice in some of the convents, like that at Quedlinburg and elsewhere. And in truth all monasteries and convents ought to be so free that God is served freely and not under compulsion. Later on, however, they became obsessed with vows and made of them an eternal prison. Consequently, these monastic vows are more highly regarded than the vows of baptism.[89] We see, hear, read, and learn more and more about the fruit of all this every day.

I can well suppose that this advice of mine will be regarded as the height of foolishness, but I am not concerned about that at the moment. I advise what seems good to me; let those who will reject it. I see for myself how the vows are

ʳ Cf. Judg. 2:6-23.

87. This is a prominent theme in Luther's views on monasticism; see his treatise *The Judgment of Martin Luther on Monastic Vows* (1521), in LW 44:312–13, 355, 367.

88. St. Agnes of Rome, fourth-century virgin and martyr (cf. LW 45:312). According to legend, the thirteen-year-old Agnes was on her way home from school when she encountered the young man who, incensed by her rejection of his passionate advances, made the false accusations that led to her martyrdom.

89. Most medieval theologians maintained that monastic vows conveyed the same grace as baptism; see, e.g., Thomas Aquinas (1225–1274), *Summa Theologica* II.2, q. 189, a. 3 ad 3. The same theologians drew a distinction between "precepts of the gospel" (the observance of which was necessary to salvation) and "counsels of perfection" (the observance of which, especially in monastic life, enabled one to achieve salvation "better and more quickly"). See Bonaventure (1221–1274), *Breviloquium* V.9, and Aquinas, *Summa Theologica* II.2, q. 108, a. 4. Luther attacks this notion in *The Treatise on Good Works* (see above, p. 267).

kept, especially the vow of chastity. This vow has become universal in these monasteries, and yet it was never commanded by Christ. On the contrary, chastity is given to very few, as he himself says [Matt. 19:11-12], as well as St. Paul [1 Cor. 7:7]. It is my heartfelt wish that everybody be helped and that Christian souls not become entangled in self-contrived human traditions and laws.

14. We also see how the priesthood has fallen, and how many a poor priest is overburdened with wife and child, his conscience troubled. Yet no one does anything to help him, though he could easily be helped. Though pope and bishops may let things go on as they are and allow what is heading for ruin to go to ruin, yet I will redeem my conscience and open my mouth freely, whether it vexes pope, bishop, or anybody else. And this is what I say: according to the institution of Christ and the apostles, every city should have a priest or bishop, as St. Paul clearly says in Titus 1[:5]. And this priest should not be compelled to live without a wedded wife but should be permitted to have one, as St. Paul writes in 1 Tim. 3[:2, 4] and Titus 1[:6-7], saying, "A bishop shall be a man who is blameless, and the husband of but one wife, whose children are obedient and well behaved," etc. According to St. Paul, and also St. Jerome, a bishop and a priest are one and the same thing.[s] But of bishops as they now are the Scriptures know nothing. They have, rather, been established by an ordinance of the Christian community, so that one priest will have authority over many others.

So then, we clearly learn from the Apostle that it should be the practice in Christendom for every town to choose from among the community a learned and pious citizen,

The martyrdom of St. Agnes.

---

s   For St. Paul, cf. Luther's interpretation of 1 Cor. 4:1 in *Concerning the Ministry* (1523), LW 40:35. For St. Jerome (c. 347–420), see his *Commentary on Titus* (PL 26:52) and *Epistulae* 146 (PL 22:1192–95).

entrust to him the office of the ministry, and support him at the expense of the community. He should be free to marry or not. He should have several priests or deacons, also free to marry or not as they choose, to help him minister to the masses and the community with word and sacrament, as is still the practice in the Greek church. Because there was afterwards so much persecution and controversy with heretics, there were many holy fathers who voluntarily abstained from matrimony so that they might better devote themselves to study and be prepared at any moment for death and conflict.

But the Roman See has interfered and out of its own wanton wickedness turned this into a universal commandment that forbade priests to marry.[90] This was done at the bidding of the devil, as St. Paul declares in 1 Tim. 4[:1, 3], "There shall come teachers who bring the devil's teaching and forbid marriage." Unfortunately so much misery has arisen from this that tongue could never tell it. Moreover, this gave the Greek church cause to separate,[91] and discord, sin, shame, and scandal were increased to no end. But this always happens when the devil starts and carries on. What, then, shall we do about it?

My advice is to restore freedom to everybody and leave every man the free choice to marry or not to marry. But then there would have to be a very different kind of government and regulation of church property; the whole canon law would have to be demolished; and few benefices could be allowed to get into Roman hands. I fear that greed is a cause of this wretched, unchaste celibacy. As a result, everyone has wanted to become a priest and everyone wants his son to study for the priesthood, not with the idea of living in chastity, for that could be done outside the priesthood, but rather to provide themselves with temporal livelihood without work or worry, contrary to God's command in Gen. 3[:19] that "in the sweat of your face you shall eat your bread." The Romanists have artfully decorated this text to mean that their labor is to pray and say Mass.

I here take no account of popes, bishops, cathedral canons, and monks, whose offices were not instituted by God.

90. The earliest papal proscription of clerical marriage dates back to the fourth century, but a serious effort at enforcing clerical celibacy in the Western church began only in the eleventh century. It reached its apex in the twelfth century, when the first and second Lateran councils (1123 and 1139) made clerical marriage not only unlawful but invalid, which meant that all sexual relations between a priest and a woman, whether they were married or not, was classed as fornication, and their children were illegitimate. The decrees of the Lateran council were incorporated into canon law, despite which clerical concubinage remained common. See James A. Brundage, *Law, Sex, and Christian Society in Medieval Europe* (Chicago: University of Chicago Press, 1987), 214–23, 251–53, 401–5, 474–77, 536–39.

91. In the Eastern church, priests and deacons can marry before ordination (though not afterward), but bishops must remain celibate. This was a point of contention between the Eastern and Western churches, but not one of the major issues in the Great Schism (1054) between them.

They have taken these burdens upon themselves, so they themselves will have to bear them. I want to speak only of the ministry that God has instituted, which consists of presiding over a community with word and sacrament, living among them, and maintaining a household. The same should be given liberty by a Christian council to marry to avoid temptation and sin. For since God has not bound them, no one else may or should bind them, even if he were an angel from heaven,[t] let alone a pope. Everything that canon law decrees to the contrary is mere fable and blather.

Furthermore, my advice to anyone henceforth being ordained a priest or anything else is that he in no wise vow to the bishop that he will remain celibate. On the contrary, he should tell the bishop that he has no right whatsoever to require such a vow, and that it is a devilish tyranny to require it. But if anyone is compelled to say, or even wants to say, *"so far as human frailty permits,"* as indeed many do, let him frankly interpret these same words in a negative manner to mean *"I do not promise chastity."* For *not human frailty* but only *the strength of angels and the power of heaven permit chaste living.*[u] In this way, a person should keep the conscience free of all vows.

I will advise neither for nor against marrying or remaining single. I leave that to a common Christian ordinance and to everyone's better judgment. I will not conceal my real opinion or withhold comfort from that pitiful band who with wives and children have fallen into disgrace and whose consciences are burdened because people call their wives priests' whores and their children priests' bastards. I say this freely by virtue of my right as court jester.[92]

You will find many a pious priest against whom nobody has anything to say except that he is weak and has come to shame with a woman, even though from the bottom of their hearts both are of a mind to live together in lawful wedded

92. The role in which Luther had cast himself in the introductory letter to Amsdorf; see above, pp. 377–78.

---

t   Cf. Gal. 1:8.

u   The italicized words are in Latin in the original and reflect Luther's ironic reference to monastic and ordination vows, always recited in Latin.

love, if they could do it with a clear conscience. But even though they both have to bear public shame, the two are certainly married in the sight of God. And I say that where they are so minded and live together, they should unburden their consciences. Let the priest take and keep her as his lawful wedded wife and live honestly with her as her husband, whether the pope likes it or not, whether it be against canon or human law. The salvation of your soul is more important than the observance of tyrannical, arbitrary, and wanton laws, which are neither necessary to salvation nor commanded by God. You should do as the children of Israel did who stole from the Egyptians the wages they had earned[v] or as a servant who steals from his wicked master the wages he has earned: steal from the pope your wedded wife and child! Let the man who has faith enough to venture this boldly follow my advice. I shall not lead him astray. Though I do not have the authority of a pope, I do have the authority of a Christian to advise and help my neighbor against sins and temptations—and that not without [good] cause or reason!

First, not every priest can do without a woman, not only because of human frailty, but much more because of keeping house. If he may have a woman [for keeping house], which the pope allows, and yet may not have her in marriage, what is that but leaving a man and a woman alone together and yet forbidding them to fall? It is just like putting straw and fire together and forbidding them to smoke or burn.

Second, the pope has as little power to command celibacy as he has to forbid eating, drinking, the natural movement of the bowels, or growing fat. Therefore, no one is bound to obey such a command, and the pope is responsible for all the sins that are committed against it, for all the souls that are lost, and for all the consciences that are confused and tortured because of it. He has strangled so many wretched souls with this devilish rope that he has long deserved to be driven out of this world. Yet it is my firm belief that God has been more gracious to many souls at their last hour than the

---

v   Cf. Exod. 12:35-36.

93. Because it was a sacrament, marriage was entirely a matter of church law that had to be adjudicated in ecclesiastical courts. The most common impediment to marriage was too close a degree of consanguinity (within the first four degrees), which meant, for example, that second cousins could not legally marry. Even the relationship between godparents and godchildren was defined as a forbidden degree of "spiritual consanguinity." Dispensations from these impediments were readily available to those who could pay for them.

94. Having dealt with the mendicant friars above (pp. 421–22), Luther now turns to monks and nuns, such as Benedictines and Cistercians, who lived by the Rule of St. Benedict.

pope was to them in their whole lifetime. No good has ever come nor will come out of the papacy and its laws.

Third, even though the law of the pope is against it, it is nonetheless the case that when a marriage is entered into against the pope's law, then his law is already at an end and is no longer valid. For God's commandment, which enjoins that no man shall put husband and wife asunder [Matt. 19:6], is above the pope's law. And the commandments of God must not be broken or neglected because of the pope's commandment. Nevertheless, many foolish jurists, along with the pope, have devised impediments and thereby prevented, broken, and brought confusion to the estate of matrimony, so that God's commandment concerning it has altogether disappeared.[93] Need I say more? In the entire canon law of the pope there are not even two lines that could instruct a devout Christian, and, unfortunately, there are so many mistaken and dangerous laws that nothing would be better than to make a bonfire of it.[w]

But if you say that [clerical marriage] is scandalous, and that the pope must first grant dispensation, I reply that whatever scandal there is in it is the fault of the Roman See, which has established such laws with no right and against God. In the sight of God and the Holy Scriptures marriage of the clergy is no offense. Moreover, if the pope can grant dispensations from his greedy and tyrannical laws for money, then every Christian can grant dispensations from these very same laws for God's sake and for the salvation of souls. For Christ has set us free from all humanly devised laws, especially when they are opposed to God and the salvation of souls, as St. Paul teaches in Gal. 5[:1] and 1 Cor. 10[:23].

15. Nor must I forget the poor monasteries.[94] The evil spirit, who has now confused all the estates of life and made them unbearable through human laws, has taken possession of some abbots, abbesses, and prelates. As a result, they govern their brothers and sisters in such a way that they quickly go to hell and lead a wretched existence here and now, as do all the devil's martyrs. That is to say, these supe-

w   This is exactly what Luther did; see p. 383, n. 15.

riors have reserved to themselves in confession all, or at least some, of the mortal sins that are secret, so that no brother can absolve another, on pain of excommunication. Now then, we do not find angels at all times and in all places, but also flesh and blood, which would rather undergo all excommunications and threats rather than confess secret sins to prelates and appointed confessors. Thus these people go to the sacrament with such consciences that they become irregulars and even worse.[95] O blind shepherds! O mad prelates! O ravenous wolves!

To this I say: if a sin is public or notorious, then it is proper for the prelate alone to punish it, and it is only these sins and no others that he may reserve and select for himself. He has no authority over secret sins, even if they were the worst sins that ever are or can be found. If the prelate reserves them, then he is a tyrant. He has no such right and is trespassing upon the prerogative of God's judgment.

And so I advise these children, brothers and sisters: if your superiors are unwilling to permit you to confess your secret sins to whomever you choose, then take them to your brother or sister, whomever you like, and be absolved and comforted. Then go and do what you want and ought to do. Only believe firmly that you are absolved, and nothing more is needed. And do not be distressed or driven mad by threats of excommunication, being made irregular, or whatever else they threaten. These [penalties] are valid only in the case of public or notorious sins that no one will confess. They do not apply to you. What are you trying to do, you blind prelates, prevent secret sins by threats? Relinquish what you obviously cannot hold on to so that God's judgment and grace may work in the people under your care! He has not given them so entirely into your hands as to let them go entirely out of his own! In fact, you have the smaller part under you. Let your statutes be merely statutes. Do not exalt them to heaven or give them the weight of divine judgments!

16. It is also necessary to abolish completely the celebration of anniversary Masses for the dead,[96] or at least to reduce their number, since we plainly see that they have become

95. Irregulars were monks who had violated the *regula* (rule) of their order and were no longer members in good standing.

96. I.e., Masses said for the repose of the souls of one or more persons on the anniversary (or appointed day of remembrance) of their deaths. Endowments were commonly provided for this purpose.

97. Endowed Masses for departed members were particularly popular with religious fraternities, and Luther had already voiced criticism of the immoderate eating and drinking that accompanied their celebration; see *Sermon on the Blessed Sacrament,* pp. 249–53.

98. Vigils were preparatory observances (prayers, Scripture readings, etc.) on the eve (or the entire day) before a major church festival, or they were prayers or observances said throughout the night as a special religious discipline, which is the sense in which Luther is using the word.

nothing but a mockery. God is deeply angered by these, and their only purpose is money-grubbing, gluttony, and drunkenness.[97] What pleasure can God take in wretched vigils and Masses that are so miserably rattled off and neither read nor prayed.[98] And if they were prayed, it would not be for God's sake and out of love, but for the sake of money and of getting the job done. But it is impossible for a work that is not done out of unconstrained love to please God or secure anything from him. So it is altogether Christian to abolish, or at least to diminish, everything we see that is becoming an abuse and that angers God rather than appeases him. I would rather—in fact, it would be more pleasing to God and much better—that a chapter, church, or monastery combine all its anniversary Masses and vigils and on one day, with sincerity of heart, reverence, and faith, hold one true vigil and Mass on behalf of all its benefactors, than hold thousands every year for each individual benefactor without reverence and faith. O dear Christians, God does not care for much praying but for true praying. In fact, he condemns long and repetitious prayers, and says in Matt. 6[:7; 23:14], "They will only earn the more punishment thereby." But Avarice, which cannot put its trust in God, brings such things to pass, for it fears that it will die of hunger.

17. Certain penalties or punishments of canon law should be abolished, too, especially the interdict,[x] which without any doubt was invented by the evil spirit. Is it not a devilish work to correct one sin through many and great sins? It is actually a greater sin to silence or suppress the word and worship of God than if one had strangled twenty popes at one time, to say nothing of a priest, or had appropriated church property. This is another of the tender virtues taught in canon law. One of the reasons this law is called "spiritual" is that it comes from "the spirit": not from the Holy Spirit but from the evil spirit.

Excommunication must never be used except where the Scriptures prescribe its use, that is, against those who do not

---

x   See above, p. 386, n. 22.

hold the true faith or who live in open sin, but not for mate-rial advantage. But today it is the other way around. Every-body believes and lives as he pleases, especially those who use excommunication to fleece and defame other people. All the excommunications are for material advantage, for which we have nobody to thank but the holy canon law of unrighteousness. I have said more about this in an earlier discourse.[y]

The other punishments and penalties—suspension, irreg-ularity, aggravation, reaggravation, deposition,[99] lightning, thundering, cursings, damnings, and the rest of these devices—should be buried ten fathoms deep in the earth so that their name and memory not be left on earth. The evil spirit unleashed by canon law has brought such a terrible plague and misery into the heavenly kingdom of holy Chris-tendom, having done nothing but destroy and hinder souls by canon law, that the words of Christ in Matt. 23[:13] may well be understood as applying to them, "Woe to you scribes! You have taken upon yourselves the authority to teach and have closed the kingdom of heaven to the people, for you do not enter and you stand in the way of those who go in."

18. All festivals should be abolished, and Sunday alone retained. If it were desired, however, to retain the festivals of Our Lady and of the major saints, they should be transferred to [the nearest] Sunday, or observed only by a morning Mass, after which all the rest of the day should be a working day. Here is the reason: since the feast days are abused by drinking, gambling, loafing, and all manner of sin, we anger God more on holy days than we do on other days.[z] Things are so topsy-turvy that holy days are not holy, but working days are. Nor is any service rendered God and his saints by so many saints' days. On the contrary, they are dishonored;

99. For "irregularity," see above, n. 95. "Aggravation" was the threat of excommunication; "reaggravation" was the excommunication itself. "Deposition" was permanent dismissal from clerical office, as opposed to temporary "suspension."

---

y   In the *Sermon on the Power of Excommunication*, published in Latin in 1518 (WA 1:638–43), and in the *Sermon on the Ban*, preached in German in December 1519 and published early in 1520 (LW 39:5–22).

z   Cf. Luther's similar observations concerning the excessive number and riotous celebration of saints' days in the *Treatise on Good Works*, p. 321.

100. Otilie (Odilia), feast day 13 December (c. 662–c. 720), was the patron saint of Alsace, and her shrine at Odilienberg was a well-known place of pilgrimage. The much more widely known and venerated St. Barbara (feast day 4 December) was the patron saint of gunners, miners, and others who work with explosives. See the *Treatise on Good Works* (p. 317, n. 82).

101. The anniversary of the consecration of a church, to which often a special indulgence was attached, was a feast day in that parish. The frequently raucous and disorderly celebration of these local feast days was a common topic of complaint from clerical reformers and public officials. See the *Explanations of the 95 Theses* (1518), LW 31:198.

although some foolish prelates think that they have done a good work if each, following the promptings of his own blind devotion, celebrates a festival in honor of St. Otilie or St. Barbara.[100] But they would be doing something far better if they honored the saint by turning the saint's day into a working day.

Over and above the spiritual injury, the average man incurs two material disadvantages from this practice. First, he neglects his work and spends more money that he would otherwise spend. Second, he weakens his body and makes it less fit. We see this every day, yet nobody thinks of correcting the situation. In such cases, we ought not to consider whether or not the pope has instituted the feasts, or whether we must have a dispensation or permission [to omit them]. Every community, town council, or government not only has the right, without the knowledge and consent of the pope or bishop, to abolish what is opposed to God and injurious to men's bodies and souls, but indeed is bound, at the risk of the salvation of its souls to abolish it, even though popes and bishops, who ought to be the first to do so, do not consent.

Above all, we ought to abolish completely all church anniversary celebrations, since they have become nothing but taverns, fairs, and gambling places, and only increase the dishonoring of God and foster the damnation of souls.[101] It does not help matters to boast that these festivals had a good beginning and are a good work. Did not God set aside his own law, which he had given from heaven, when it was perverted and abused? And does he not daily overturn what he has set up and destroy what he has made because of the same perversion and abuse? As it is written of him in Ps. 18[:26], "You show yourself perverse with the perverted."

19. The grades or degrees within which marriage is forbidden, such as those affecting godparents or the third and fourth degree of kinship,*a* should be changed. If the pope in Rome can grant dispensations and scandalously sell them for money, then every priest may give the same dispensations

a   See above, n. 93.

without charge and for the salvation of souls. Would God that every priest were able to do and remit without payment all those things we have to pay for at Rome, such as indulgences, letters of indulgence, butter letters, Mass letters, and all the rest of the *confessionalia* and skullduggery at Rome[102] and free us from that golden noose, canon law, by which the poor people are deceived and cheated of their money! If the pope has the right to sell his noose of gold and his spiritual snares (I ought to say "law")[b] for money, then a priest certainly has more right to tear these nooses and snares apart, and for God's sake tread them underfoot. But if the priest does not have this right, neither does the pope have the right to sell them at his disgraceful fair.

Furthermore, fasts should be left to individual choice and every kind of food made optional, as the gospel makes them.[c] Even those gentlemen at Rome scoff at the fasts and leave us commoners to eat the fat they would not deign to use to grease their shoes, and then afterward they sell us the liberty to eat butter and all sorts of other things. The holy Apostle says that we already have freedom in all these things through the gospel.[d] But they have bound us with their canon law and robbed us of our rights so that we have to buy them back again with money. In so doing they have made our consciences so timid and fearful that it is no longer easy to preach about liberty of this kind because the common people take offense at it and think that eating butter is a greater sin than lying, swearing, or even living unchastely. Do with it what you will, it is still a human work decreed by human beings, and nothing good will ever come of it.

20. The chapels in forests and the churches in fields,[103] such as Wilsnack,[104] Sternberg,[105] Trier,[106] the Grimmenthal,[107] and now Regensburg[108] and a goodly number of others that recently have become the goal of pilgrimages, must be leveled. Oh, what a terrible and heavy reckoning

---

102. For indulgences and butter letters, see above, p. 406, n. 60 [*Butterbriefe*]. Mass letters (*messbriefe*) were certificates entitling the bearer to the benefits of Masses celebrated by confraternities. See above, p. 229, n. 3.

103. Chapels built in the countryside as goals of pilgrimage, not as parish churches.

104. Bad Wilsnack in Brandenburg became a pilgrimage site after 1384, when three consecrated hosts (communion wafers) reportedly survived a fire undamaged and with a drop of Christ's blood in each.

105. From 1491 the Augustinian monastery at Sternberg in Mecklenberg was a popular goal of pilgrims because of a "bleeding host" (consecrated bread) displayed there.

106. The cathedral at Trier possessed one of the many cloaks claiming to be the seamless robe of Christ for which his executioners had cast lots (John 19:23-24).

107. Grimmenthal (near Meiningen) had a pilgrimage church (rebuilt and expanded 1499–1507) with a statue of the Virgin Mary that was said to effect miraculous cures.

108. In 1519, when the Jews were expelled from Regensburg, the synagogue was torn down and replaced with a chapel dedicated to the Virgin Mary. "The Fair Virgin of Regensburg," a painting in the chapel, quickly became an object of veneration and pilgrimage.

---

b   Luther makes an untranslatable pun on *geistliche netz* ("spiritual snares") and *geistlich recht* ("spiritual law" = canon law).

c   Cf. Matt. 15:11.

d   1 Cor. 10:23; Col. 2:16.

The pilgrimage shrine of St. Mary's in Regensburg, built on the site of a recently destroyed synagogue. Woodcut by Michael Ostendorfer (c. 1490–1559).

those bishops will have to give who permit this devilish deceit and profit by it. They should be the first to prevent it, and yet they regard it all as a godly and holy thing. They do not see that the devil is behind it all, to strengthen greed, to create a false and fictitious faith, to weaken the parish churches, to multiply taverns and whoring, to lose money and working time to no purpose, and to lead ordinary people by the nose. If they had read Scripture as well as the damnable canon law, they would know how to deal with this matter!

The miracles that happen in these places prove nothing, for the evil spirit can also work miracles, as Christ has told us in Matt. 24[:24]. If they took the matter seriously and forbade this sort of thing, the miracles would quickly come to an end. But if the thing were of God, their prohibition would not hinder it.[e] And if there were no other evidence that it is not of God, the fact that people come running to them like herds of cattle, as if they had lost all reason, would be proof enough. This could not be possible if it were of God. Further, since God never gave any command about all this, there is neither obedience nor merit in doing it. Therefore one should step in boldly and protect the people. For whatever has not been commanded and is done beyond what God commands is certainly the devil's doing. It also works to the disadvantage of parish churches, because they are held in less respect. In short, these things are signs of great unbelief among the people, for if they really had faith they would find all they need in their own parish churches, to which they are commanded to go.

e   Acts 5:39.

But what shall I say now? Every bishop thinks only of how he can set up and maintain such a place of pilgrimage in his diocese. He is not at all concerned that the people believe and live aright. The rulers are just like the people. The blind lead the blind [Luke 6:39]. In fact, where pilgrimages do not catch on, they set to work to canonize saints, not to honor the saints, who would be honored enough without being canonized, but to draw the crowds and bring in the money. At this point, pope and bishops lend their aid. There is a deluge of indulgences. There is always money enough for these. But nobody worries about what God has commanded. Nobody runs after these things; nobody has money for them. How blind we are! We not only give the devil free rein for his mischief, but we even strengthen and multiply his mischief. I would rather the dear saints were left in peace and the simple people not led astray! What spirit gave the pope authority to canonize saints? Who tells him whether they are saints or not? Are there not enough sins on earth already without tempting God, without interfering in his judgment and setting up the dear saints as decoys to get money?

My advice is to let the saints canonize themselves. Indeed, it is God alone who should canonize them. And let all stay in their own parishes, where they will find more than in all the shrines even if they were all rolled into one. In one's own parish one finds baptism, the sacrament, preaching, and one's neighbor, and these things are greater than all the saints in heaven, for all of them were made "saints" by God's word and sacrament. As long as we esteem such wonderful things so little, God is just in his wrathful condemnation in allowing the devil to lead us where he likes, to conduct pilgrimages, found churches and chapels, canonize saints, and do other such fool's works, so that we depart from true faith into a novel and wrong kind of belief. This is what the devil did in ancient times to the people of Israel, when he led them away from the temple at Jerusalem to countless other places. Yet he did it all in the name of God and under the pretense of holiness. All the prophets preached against it, and they were martyred for doing so. But today nobody preaches against it. If somebody were to preach against it all, perhaps bishop,

109. Antoninus (1389–1459), archbishop of Florence, achieved renown as reformer of the Dominican order. When Luther wrote this treatise, the procedure of canonizing Antoninus (completed in 1523) was already under way.

110. An indult is a permission or a privilege, awarded to an individual or group by competent ecclesiastical authority (the pope or a bishop), granting exemption from a particular norm of canon law.

111. "Faculties" were extraordinary powers to grant indulgences and absolution in reserved cases. They were usually bestowed on papal legates or commissioners but could be bestowed on local church officials.

pope, priest, and monk would possibly martyr him, too. St. Antoninus of Florence[109] and certain others must now be made saints and canonized in this way, so that their holiness, which would otherwise have served only for the glory of God and set a good example, may be used to bring fame and money.

Although the canonization of saints may have been a good thing in former days, it is certainly never good practice now, just as many other things that were good in former times—feast days, church treasures and ornaments—are now scandalous and offensive. For it is evident that through the canonization of saints neither God's glory nor the improvement of Christians is sought, but only money and reputation. One church wants to have the advantage over the other and would not like to see another church enjoy that advantage in common. In these last evil days spiritual treasures have even been misused to gain temporal goods, so that everything, even God himself, has been forced into the service of Avarice. This only promotes schisms, sects, and pride. A church that has advantages over others looks down on them and exalts itself. Yet all divine treasures are common to all and serve all and ought to further the cause of unity. But the pope likes things as they are. He would not like it if all Christians were equal and one with each other.

It is fitting to say here that all church privileges, bulls, and whatever else the pope sells in that skinning house of his in Rome should be abolished, disregarded, or extended to all. But if he sells or gives indults,[110] privileges, indulgences, graces, advantages, and faculties[111] to Wittenberg, Halle, Venice, and above all to his own city of Rome, why does he not give these things to all churches in general? Is it not his duty to do everything in his power for all Christians, freely and for God's sake, even to shed his blood for them? Tell me, then, why does he give or sell to one church and not to another? Or must the accursed money make so great a difference in the eyes of His Holiness among Christians, who all have the same baptism, word, faith, Christ, God, and all else?[f] Do the Romanists want us to be so blind to all these things, though we have eyes to see, and be such fools, though we have a perfectly good faculty of reason, that we worship such greed, skullduggery, and pretense?[g] The pope is your shepherd, but only so long as you have money and no longer. And still the Romanists are not ashamed of this rascality of leading us hither and thither with their bulls. They are concerned only about the accursed money and nothing else!

My advice is this: If such fool's work is not abolished, then all upright Christians[h] should open their eyes and not permit themselves to be led astray by the Romanist bulls and seals and all their glittering show. Let them stay at home in their own parish church and let their baptism, their gospel, faith, Christ, and God, who is the same God everywhere, be what is best to them. Let the pope remain a blind leader of the blind.[i] Neither an angel nor a pope can give you as much as God gives you in your parish church. Indeed, the pope leads you away from God's gifts, which are yours for free, to his gifts, for which you have to pay. He gives you lead for gold, hide for meat, the string for the purse, wax for honey, words for goods, the letter for the spirit.[112] You see all this before your very eyes, but you refuse to take notice. If you intend to ride to heaven on his wax and parchment, this chariot will soon break down and you will fall into hell, and not in God's name![j]

Let this be your one sure rule. Whatever you have to buy from the pope is neither good nor from God. For what God gives is not only given without charge, but the whole world is punished and damned for not being willing to receive it as a free gift. I am talking about the gospel and God's work. We have deserved God's letting us be so led astray because we have despised his holy word and the grace of baptism. It is as St. Paul says, "God shall send a strong delusion upon all those who have not received the truth to their salvation, so

112. The imagery here is that of a papal bull, which was written on parchment (animal hide) and to which was attached with wax a cord from which the seal hung. For "letter and spirit," see 2 Cor. 3:6.

f   Cf. Eph. 4:4-6.
g   German: *Spiegelfechten*, literally, "standing in front of a mirror and pretending to fight"; in other words, being pretentious, hypocritical, or phony.
h   Singular in the original.
i   Cf. Matt. 15:14.
j   Echoing 2 Kgs. 2:1-12.

113. Luther is breaking with the medieval tradition, in which begging was a respectable activity for those who had fallen into poverty or for those who, like mendicant friars and pilgrims, chose to support themselves in that fashion. By the early sixteenth century, urban populations increasingly viewed the large numbers of beggars as a threat to good order. While Catholic authorities sought to regulate begging, Protestant authorities outlawed it and established laws and institutions for the care of the poor. By 1522, for example, Wittenberg had outlawed begging and established a Poor Chest Ordinance. In the following year, Luther provided a preface for the *Ordinance of a Common Chest* enacted by the Saxon town of Leisnig (LW 45:161-94).

114. Luther's word is *botschafften* ("messengers" or "ambassadors"). The reference is to the so-called *stationarii* (*stationirer* in German), members of religious orders who exploited the gullibility of peasants and villagers by enrolling them, in return for an annual fee, on lists of beneficiaries of the intercession of the saint whose messenger they claimed to be (e.g., St. Valentine). The supposed benefit derived was freedom from certain diseases (epilepsy in the case of Valentine). See Benrath, 105-6, n. 79, and cf. p. 441, note *m*.

that they believe and follow lies and knavery" [2 Thess. 2:11], as they deserve.

21. One of the greatest necessities is the abolition of all begging in all of Christendom. Nobody ought to go begging among Christians. It would indeed be a very simple matter to make a law to the effect that every city should look after its own poor, if only we had the courage and the intention to do so.[113] No beggar from outside should be allowed into the city, whether he call himself pilgrim or mendicant monk. Every city should support its own poor, and if it was too small, the people in the surrounding villages should also be urged to contribute, since in any case they have to feed so many vagabonds and evil rogues who call themselves mendicants. In this way, too, it could be known who was really poor and who was not.

There would have to be an overseer or warden who knows all the poor and informs the city council or the clergy what they needed. Or some other better arrangement might be made. As I see it, there is no other business in which so much skullduggery and deceit are practiced as in begging, and yet it could all be easily abolished. Moreover, this unrestricted universal begging is harmful to the common people. I have figured out that each of the five or six mendicant orders[k] visits the same place more than six or seven times every year. In addition to these, there are the common beggars, the ambassador beggars,[114] and the pilgrims. This adds up to sixty times a year that a town is laid under tribute. This is over and above what the secular authorities demand in the way of taxes and assessments. All this the Romanist See steals in return for its wares and consumes for no purpose. To me it is one of God's greatest miracles that we can still go on existing and find the wherewithal to support ourselves.

To be sure, some think that if these proposals were adopted the poor would not be so well provided for, that fewer great stone houses and monasteries would be built, and fewer so well furnished. I can well believe all this. But none of it is necessary. Whoever has chosen poverty ought

k   Franciscans, Dominicans, Augustinians, Carmelites, Servites.

not be rich. If he wants to be rich, let him put his hand to the plow and seek his fortune from the land. It is enough if the poor are decently cared for so that they do not die of hunger or cold. It is not fitting that one person should live in idleness on another's labor, or be rich and live comfortably at the cost of another's hardship, as it is according to the present perverted custom. St. Paul says, "Whoever will not work shall not eat" [2 Thess. 3:10]. God has not decreed that anyone shall live off the property of another, save only the clergy who preach and have a parish to care for, and they should, as St. Paul says in 1 Corinthians 9[:14], on account of their spiritual labor. And also as Christ says to the apostles, "Every laborer is worthy of his wage" [Luke 10:7].

22. It is also to be feared that the many Masses that have been endowed in ecclesiastical foundations[115] and monasteries are not only of little use, but arouse the great wrath of God. It would therefore be beneficial to endow no more of such Masses, but rather to abolish the many that are already endowed. It is obvious that these Masses are regarded only as sacrifices and good works, even though they are sacraments just like baptism and penance, which profit only those who receive them and no one else. But now the custom of saying Masses for the living and the dead has crept in, and all things are based on them. This is why so many Masses are endowed, and why the state of affairs that we see has developed out of it.

But this is perhaps a too bold and an unheard-of proposal, especially for those who are concerned that they would lose their job and means of livelihood if such Masses were discontinued. I must refrain from saying more about it until we arrive again at a proper understanding of what the Mass is and what it is for. Unfortunately, for many years now it has been a job, a way to earn a living. Therefore, from now on I will advise a person to become a shepherd or some sort of workman rather than a priest or a monk, unless he knows well in advance what this celebrating of Masses is all about.

I am not speaking, however, of the old collegiate foundations and cathedral chapters, which were doubtless established for the sake of the children of the nobility. According

115. For example, in 1519 the All Saints' Foundation at Wittenberg's Castle Church, consisting of sixteen foundation canons, some of whom were teachers at the University of Wittenberg, recited over six thousand private Masses for the dead (mostly deceased members of the Saxon elector's family).

to German custom, not every one of a nobleman's children can become a landowner or a ruler. It was intended that these children should be looked after in such foundations, and there be free to serve God, to study, to become educated people, and to educate others. I am speaking now of the new foundations that have been established just for the saying of prayers and Masses, and because of their example the older foundations are being burdened with the same sort of praying and Mass celebrating, so that even these old foundations serve little or no purpose. And it is by the grace of God that they finally hit the bottom, as they deserve. That is to say, they have been reduced to choir singing, howling organs, and the reading of cold, indifferent Masses to get and consume the income from the endowments. Pope, bishops, and university scholars ought to be looking into these things and writing about them, and yet they are precisely the ones who do the most to promote them. Whatever brings in money they let go on and on. The blind lead the blind [Luke 6:39]. This is what greed and canon law accomplish.

It should no longer be permissible for one person to hold more than one canonry or benefice. Each must be content with a modest position so that someone else may also have something. This would do away with the excuses of those who say that they must hold more than one such office to maintain their proper station [in life]. A proper station could be interpreted in such broad terms that an entire country would not be enough to maintain it. But greed and a mistrust of God go hand in hand in this matter, so that what is alleged to be the needs of a proper station is nothing but greed and mistrust.

23. Brotherhoods,[116] and for that matter, indulgences, letters of indulgence, butter letters, Mass letters, dispensations, and everything of that kind,[l] should be snuffed out and brought to an end. There is nothing good about them. If the pope has the authority to grant you a dispensation to eat butter, to absent yourself from Mass and the like, then he ought also to be able to delegate this authority to priests,

116. Brotherhoods (*bruderschaften*)—also known as fraternities, sodalities, religious guilds, and (most often in English) confraternities—were associations of laymen created for the purpose of promoting the religious life of their members. Any town of any size had several; in 1520 Wittenberg had twenty. Frequently certain indulgences were attached to membership and attendance at Masses or other rituals at appointed times. Great importance was attached to the endowment of Masses for the souls of departed members. Although brotherhoods could become deeply involved in the charitable and cultural as well as the religious life of their communities, they were often criticized, in Germany at any rate, as drinking clubs whose members missed no opportunity for gluttony and drunkenness. Luther's jaundiced view of them is more fully expressed in his *Sermon on the Blessed Sacrament*, pp. 249–53 above. Cf. Benrath, 105–6, n. 79.

l   See nn. 55, 59, 60, and 102.

from whom he had no right to take it in the first place. I am speaking especially of those brotherhoods in which indulgences, Masses, and good works are apportioned. My dear friend, in your baptism you have entered into a brotherhood with Christ, with all the angels, with the saints, and with all Christians on earth. Hold fast to these and do right by them, and you will have brotherhoods enough. Let the others glitter as they will, compared with the true brotherhood in Christ those brotherhoods are like a penny compared with a gulden. But if there were a brotherhood that raised money to feed the poor or to help the needy, that would be a good idea. It would find its indulgences and its merits in heaven. But today nothing comes of these groups except gluttony and drunkenness.

Above all, we should drive out of German territory the papal legates*m* with their faculties,*n* which they sell to us for large sums of money. This traffic is nothing but skullduggery. For example, for the payment of money they make unrighteousness into righteousness, and they dissolve oaths, vows, and agreements, thereby destroying and teaching us to destroy the faith and fealty that have been pledged. They assert that the pope has authority to do this. It is the devil who tells them to say these things. They sell us doctrine so satanic, and take money for it, that they are teaching us sin and leading us to hell.

If there were no other base trickery to prove that the pope is the true Antichrist, this one would be enough to prove it. Hear this, O pope, not of all men the holiest but of all men the most sinful! O that God from heaven would soon destroy your throne and sink it in the abyss of hell! Who has given you authority to exalt yourself above your God, to violate and "loosen"[117] what he has commanded, and teach Christians, especially the German nation, praised throughout history for its nobility, constancy, and fidelity, to be inconstant, perjurers, traitors, profligates, and faithless?

117. A play on the power to bind and loose sins, first given to Peter (Matt. 16:19) and claimed by later popes as their exclusive right.

---

m The word again is *botschafften*, but here it appears to mean not the *stationarii* of n. 114 but, rather, actual papal commissioners.

n See n. 111.

118. In 1443 Vladislaus III, king of Poland (1424-1444) and (as Uladislaus I) king of Hungary, signed at Szeged a ten-year truce with the Turks. In the following year, Vladislaus allowed himself to be persuaded by the papal legate, Cardinal Cesarini (1398-1444), that the truce was invalid because the Turks could not be trusted to keep their word. So he renewed the war, as a result of which both he and the legate were killed at the battle of Varna on 10 November 1444.

119. Like Luther after him, the Bohemian reformer Jan Hus (1372-1415), lecturer at the University of Prague and popular preacher in the Bethlehem Chapel in Prague, rejected papal authority, demanded free preaching of the gospel, insisted on the right of the laity to receive communion in both kinds, and denounced clerical vices such as simony and the sale of indulgences. He was excommunicated in 1410, and when his supporters in Prague took to the streets in his defense, the city was placed under interdict (1412). Summoned to appear at the Council of Constance, Hus did so under a safe-conduct granted by Emperor Sigismund (1368-1437). But the council decreed that, according to divine and human law, no promise made to a heretic was binding. Hus was arrested, imprisoned, put on trial, and on 6 July 1415 burned at the stake. Luther is mistaken in assuming that Hus's colleague Jerome of Prague (1379-1416), who journeyed to Constance to support Hus, was also given a safe-conduct. Like Hus, he was arrested and burned at the stake.

God has commanded us to keep word and faith even with an enemy, but you have taken it upon yourself to loosen his commandment and have ordained in your heretical, anti-Christian decretals that you have his power. Thus through your voice and pen the wicked Satan lies as he has never lied before. You force and twist the Scriptures to suit your fancy. O Christ, my Lord, look down; let the day of your judgment burst forth and destroy this nest of devils at Rome. There sits the man of whom St. Paul said, "He shall exalt himself above you, sit in your church, and set himself up as God, that man of sin, the son of perdition" [2 Thess. 2:3-5]. What else is papal power but simply the teaching and increasing of sin and wickedness? Papal power serves only to lead souls into damnation in your name and, to all outward appearances, with your approval!

In ancient times the children of Israel had to keep the oath that they had unwittingly been deceived into giving to their enemies, the Gibeonites [Josh. 9:3-21]. And King Zedekiah was miserably lost along with all his people because he broke his oath to the king of Babylon [2 Kgs. 24:20—25:7]. In our own history, a hundred years ago, that fine king of Hungary and Poland, Ladislaus, was tragically slain by the Turk along with a great many of his people because he allowed himself to be led astray by the papal legate and cardinal and broke the good and advantageous treaty and solemn agreement he had made with the Turk.[118] The pious Emperor Sigismund had no more success after the Council of Constance when he allowed those scoundrels to break the oath that had been given to John Hus and Jerome.[119] All the trouble between the Bohemians and us stems from this. Even in our own times—God help us!—how much Christian blood has been shed because of the oath and the alliance which Pope Julius made between Emperor Maximilian and King Louis of France, and afterward broke![120] How could I tell all the trouble the popes have stirred up by their devilish presumption with which they annul oaths and vows made between powerful princes, making a mockery of these things, and taking money for it? I hope that the judgment day is at hand. Things could not possibly be worse than the state of

IOANNES HVSSVS BOHEMVS.
Cæsaris huic violata fides, damnatus iniquè est
Vir pius et vera relligionis amans.
Nonne (inquit) lapsos post centum iugiter annos
Danda deo ratio est impia turba tibi?
Cum priuill.

Portrait of Jan Hus (c. 1369–1415).
Engraved by Hendrik Hondius (1573–1650),
whose initial is at the upper right.

120. In 1508, Pope Julius II, King Louis XII of France, Emperor Maximilian I, and King Ferdinand of Aragon (1452–1516) formed the League of Cambrai against Venice. After the defeat of Venice at the hands of the French in 1509, Julius abandoned the League and in 1510 concluded with Ferdinand of Aragon, Emperor Maximilian, Henry VIII of England (1491–1547), and the Swiss a new alliance, the Holy League, aimed at expelling the French from Italy. This aim had been largely achieved by the death of Louis XII in 1515, but only temporarily. The Italian wars—essentially a dynastic power-struggle between the Valois of France (Francis I) and the Habsburgs of Spain and Burgundy (Charles V)—would continue, with brief periods of respite, until 1559, with frequently disastrous consequences for the papacy and the Italian states, especially with the sack of Rome in 1527 by the troops of Charles V.

121. Following the burning of Hus at Constance, the Hussite nobles and cities in Bohemia rallied to the defense of their reform movement. This led to a Hussite revolution, which five "crusades" mounted by Sigismund, Holy Roman Emperor and king of Bohemia, could not put down (1419–1431). In 1436, a peace treaty between the Council of Basel, Emperor Sigismund, and the Hussites was concluded, guaranteeing the continued existence of the Hussite communities and the right of Hussites to hold public office. Rome never officially accepted this agreement, but it remained in force in Bohemia nonetheless. This

affairs the Romanist See is promoting. The pope suppresses God's commandment and exalts his own. If he is not the Antichrist, then somebody tell me who is. But more of this another time.[o]

24. It is high time we took up the Bohemian question and dealt seriously and honestly with it.[121] We should come to an understanding with them so that the terrible slander,

[o] Luther may have been referring to his recently published tract (26 June 1520), *On the Papacy in Rome, against the Most Celebrated Romanist in Leipzig* (LW 39:49–104).

meant that there were two confessions in one Christian country: Hussites (predominantly Czech speaking) and Catholics (German speaking).

122. Because Luther denied that the pope ruled the church by divine right, his enemies had accused him of teaching "the Bohemian heresy" of Hus, a charge made by Johann Eck (1486–1543) at the Leipzig Debate in 1519. On that occasion, as here, Luther insisted that Hus had been erroneously and unjustly condemned as a heretic. See Brecht 1:319–21 and LW 31:314.

hatred, and envy on both sides comes to an end. As befits my folly, I shall be the first to submit an opinion on this subject, with due deference to everyone who may understand the case better than I.

First, we must honestly confess the truth and stop justifying ourselves. We must admit to the Bohemians that John Hus and Jerome of Prague were burned at Constance against the papal, Christian, imperial oath, and promise of safe-conduct. This happened contrary to God's commandment and gave the Bohemians ample cause for bitterness. And although they should have acted as perfect Christians and suffered this grave injustice and disobedience to God by these people, nevertheless, they were not obliged to condone such conduct and acknowledge it as just. To this day they would rather give up life and limb than admit that it is right to break and deal contrarily with an imperial, papal, and Christian oath. So then, although it is the impatience of the Bohemians that is at fault, yet the pope and his crowd are still more to blame for all the misery, error, and the loss of souls which have followed that council.

I will not pass judgment here on the articles of John Hus, or defend his errors, although I have not yet found any errors in his writings according to my way of thinking.[122] I firmly believe that those who violated a Christian safe-conduct and a commandment of God with their faithless betrayal gave neither a fair judgment nor an honest condemnation. Without doubt they were possessed more by the evil spirit than by the Holy Spirit. Nobody will doubt that the Holy Spirit does not act contrary to the commandment of God, and nobody is so ignorant as not to know that the violation of good faith and of a promise of safe-conduct is contrary to the commandment of God, even though they had been promised to the devil himself, to say nothing of a mere heretic. It is also quite evident that such a promise was made to John Hus and the Bohemians and was not kept, and that he was burnt at the stake as a result. I do not wish, however, to make John Hus a saint or a martyr, as some of the Bohemians do. But at the same time I do acknowledge that an injustice was done to him, and that his books and doctrines were unjustly condemned. For the judgments of God are secret and terrible, and no one save God alone should undertake to reveal or utter them.

I only want to say this. John Hus may have been as bad a heretic as it is possible to be, but he was burned unjustly and in violation of the commandment of God. Further, the Bohemians should not be forced to approve of such conduct, or else we shall never achieve any unity. Not obstinacy, but the open admission of the truth must make us one. It is useless to pretend, as was done at the time, that the oath of safe-conduct given to a heretic need not be kept. That is as much as to say that God's commandments need not be kept so that God's commandments may be kept. The devil made the Romanists insane and foolish so that they did not know what they had said and done. God has commanded that a promise of safe-conduct ought to be kept. We should keep such a commandment though the whole world collapses. How much more, then, when it is only a question of freeing a heretic! We should overcome heretics with books, not with fire, as the ancient fathers did. If it were wisdom to vanquish heretics with fire, then public hangmen would be the most learned scholars on earth. We would no longer need to study books, for he who overcomes another by force would have the right to burn him at the stake.

Second, the emperor and princes should send a few really upright and sensible bishops and scholars [to the Bohemians]. On no account should they send a cardinal or a papal legate or an inquisitor, for such people are most unversed in Christian things. They do not seek the salvation of souls, but, like all the pope's henchmen, only their own power, profit, and prestige. In fact, these very people were the chief actors in this miserable business at Constance. The people sent into Bohemia should find out from the Bohemians how things stand in regard to their faith, and whether it is possible to unite all their sects.[123] In this case, the pope ought, for the sake of saving souls, relinquish his power [of appointment] for a time and, in accordance with the decree of the

123. After the death of Hus, his followers divided into two groups. The more moderate group was known as the Utraquists or the Calixtines because of their demand for communion in both kinds (*sub utraque*), i.e., that the cup (*calix*) be administered to the laity. Otherwise they were essentially Catholic in doctrine. The other group, know as Taborites (after Mount Tabor, their fortified stronghold near Prague) were socially and theologically more radical and sought to extend the kingdom of God by force of arms. In the 1420s they split into two groups, the more moderate joining the Utraquists, the radicals surviving only to be annihilated on the battlefield in 1434. In the 1460s a radical group of Utraquists broke away to form the Bohemian Brethren (also known as the Unity of the Brotherhood), who rejected private property, oaths and all other civic obligations, and sought to live simple Christian lives away from urban centers. In the 1470s the Utraquists again began to splinter in two directions. A conservative faction sought to reestablish their connections with Rome, while the more radical faction, now called the New Utraquists, deliberately distanced themselves from Rome. By 1519 leaders of this group were in communication with Martin Luther. See *Oxford Encyclopedia of the Reformation*, ed. Hans Hillebrandt, 4 vols. (New York & Oxford: Oxford University Press, 1996), 1:185–86 s.v. "Bohemian Brethren"; 2:278–80, s.v. "Hussites"; and 4:206–8, s.v. "Utraquists."

truly Christian Council of Nicaea,[p] allow the Bohemians to choose an archbishop of Prague from among their number and let him be confirmed by the bishop of Olmütz in Moravia, or the bishop of Gran in Hungary, or the bishop of Gnesen in Poland, or the bishop of Magdeburg in Germany. It would be enough if he is confirmed by one or two of these, as was the custom in the time of St. Cyprian.[q] The pope has no right to oppose such an arrangement, and if he does oppose it, he will be acting like a wolf and a tyrant; no one ought to obey him, and his ban should be met with a counterban.

If, however, in deference to the chair of Peter, it were desired to do this with the pope's consent, then let it be done this way—provided that it does not cost the Bohemians a single penny and provided that the pope does not put them under the slightest obligation or bind them with his tyrannical oaths and vows as he does all other bishops, contrary to God and right. If he is not satisfied with the honor of being asked for consent, then let them not bother anymore about the pope or his vows and his rights, his laws and his tyrannies. Let the election suffice, and let the blood of all the souls endangered by this state of affairs cry out against him. No one ought to consent to what is wrong. It is enough to have shown courtesy to tyranny. If it cannot be otherwise, then an election and the approval of the common people can even now be quite as valid as confirmation by a tyrant, though I hope this will not be necessary. Someday some of the Romanists or some of the good bishops and scholars will take notice of the pope's tyranny and repudiate it.

I would also advise against compelling the Bohemians to abolish both kinds in the sacrament, since that practice is neither un-Christian nor heretical. If they want to, I would let them go on in the way they have been doing. Yet the new bishop should be careful that no discord arises because of such a practice. He should kindly instruct them that neither practice is wrong,[124] just as it ought not to cause dissension that the clergy differ from the laity in manner of life and

124. Luther defends communion in both bread and wine for the laity in *The Babylonian Captivity of the Church* (1520), LW 36:19–28, but still permitted communion in one kind, a position maintained (for the sake of the weak) in his *Invocavit* sermons, preached upon his return from Wartburg in March 1522 (LW 51:90–91) and in the *Instruction by the Visitors for the Parish Pastors of Saxony* from 1528 (LW 40:288–92).

p   See p. 409, n. 64.
q   See p. 383, n. 16.

dress. By the same token, if they were unwilling to receive Roman canon law, they should not be forced to so do, but rather the prime concern should be that they live sincerely in faith and in accordance with Holy Scripture. For Christian faith and life can well exist without the intolerable laws of the pope. In fact, faith cannot properly exist unless there are fewer or none of these Romanist laws. In baptism we have become free and have been made subject only to God's word. Why should we become bound by the word of any man? As St. Paul says, "You have become free; do not become a bond-servant of mortals,"[r] that is, of those who rule by human laws.

If I knew that the Pickards[125] held no other error regarding the sacrament of the altar except believing that the bread and wine are present in their true nature, but that the body and blood of Christ are truly present under them, then I would not condemn them but would let them come under the bishop of Prague. For it is not an article of faith that bread and wine are not present in the sacrament in their own essence and nature, but this is an opinion of St. Thomas and the pope.[126] On the other hand, it is an article of faith that the true natural body and blood of Christ are present in the natural bread and wine. So then, we should tolerate the opinions of both sides until they come to an agreement, because there is no danger in believing that the bread is there or that it is not.[s] We have to endure all sorts of practices and ordinances that are not harmful to faith. On the other hand, if they held heterodox beliefs, I would rather think of them as outside [the church], although I would teach them the truth.

Whatever other errors and schisms are discovered in Bohemia should be tolerated until the archbishop has been restored and has gradually brought all the people together again in one common doctrine. They will certainly never be united by force, defiance, or by haste. Patience and gentleness

125. Strictly speaking, the word *Pickards*, a corruption of *Beghards*, applies to the communities of pious laymen (members of corresponding sisterhoods were known as Beguines) that arose, chiefly in the Low Countries, in the twelfth and thirteenth centuries and were suspected of heresy by the ecclesiastical hierarchy. But, as here, the name was often applied to Hussites in Bohemia.

126. Since the Fourth Lateran Council of 1215, it has been official Catholic doctrine that in the Eucharist the whole substance of the bread and wine are transubstantiated into the whole substance of the body and blood of Christ, only the accidents (i.e., the outward appearances of bread and wine) remaining. The doctrine received its classical formulation from St. Thomas Aquinas, who employed the categories of substance and accidents found in Aristotelian metaphysics.

---

r   Cf. 1 Cor. 7:23; Gal. 5:1.

s   Luther's views were more fully developed in *The Babylonian Capitivity of the Church* (1520) in LW 36:28–35.

are needed here. Did not even Christ have to tarry with his disciples and bear with their unbelief for a long time until they believed his resurrection? If only the Bohemians had a regular bishop and church administration again, without Romanist tyranny, I am sure that things would soon be better.

The restoration of the temporal goods that formerly belonged to the church should not be too strictly demanded, but since we are Christians and each is bound to help the rest, we have full power to give them these things for the sake of unity and allow them to retain them in the sight of God and before the eyes of the world. For Christ says, "Where two are in agreement with one another on earth, there am I in the midst of them" [Matt. 18:19-20]. Would God that on both sides we were working toward this unity, extending to each other the hand of brotherhood and humility. Love is greater and is more needed than the papacy at Rome, which is without love. Love can exist apart from the papacy.

With this counsel I shall have done what I could. If the pope or his supporters hinder it, they shall have to render an account for having sought their own advantage rather than their neighbor's, contrary to the love of God. The pope ought to give up his papacy and all his possessions and honors, if thereby he could save one soul. But today he would rather let the whole world perish than yield one hair's-breadth of his presumptuous authority. And yet he wants to be the holiest of all! Herewith I am excused.

25. The universities, too, need a good, thorough reformation. I must say this, no matter whom it annoys. Everything the papacy has instituted and ordered serves only to increase sin and error. What else are the universities, unless they are utterly changed from what they have been hitherto, than what the book of Maccabees calls *gymnasia epheborum et graecae gloriae*?[127] What are they but places where loose living is practiced, where little is taught of the Holy Scriptures and Christian faith, and where only the blind, heathen teacher Aristotle rules far more than Christ?[128] In this regard my advice would be that Aristotle's *Physics, Metaphysics, Concerning the Soul,* and *Ethics,* which hitherto have been thought to

127. I.e., schools in which young men were taught the Greek way of life, including the worship of other gods, rather than Jewish law. Cf. 2 Macc. 4:7-17.

128. Although Luther greatly appreciated the value of Aristotle's works for the discipline of logical reasoning, he agreed with Erasmus and other humanists (not to mention some medieval scholars) that Aristotle had had a baneful influence on Scholastic theology. He took particular exception to Aristotle's teaching that human beings become good by doing good, which, in his judgment, encouraged the mistaken attribution of efficacy to human effort, apart from grace, in the process of justification.

be his best books, should be completely discarded along with all the rest of his books that boast about nature, although nothing can be learned from them either about nature or the Spirit. Moreover, nobody has yet understood him, and many souls have been burdened with fruitless labor and study, at the cost of much precious time. I dare say that any potter has more knowledge of nature than is written in these books. It grieves me to the quick that this damned, arrogant, villainous heathen has deluded and made fools of so many of the best Christians with his misleading writings. God has sent him as a plague upon us on account of our sins.

This wretched fellow in his best book, *Concerning the Soul*, even teaches that the soul dies with the body, although many have tried without success to save his reputation. As though we did not have the Holy Scriptures, in which we are fully instructed about all things, things about which Aristotle has not the faintest clue! And yet this dead heathen has conquered, obstructed, and almost succeeded in suppressing the books of the living God. When I think of this miserable business, I can only believe that the evil spirit has introduced the study [of Aristotle].

For the same reasons his *Ethics* is the worst of all books. It flatly opposes divine grace and all Christian virtues, and yet it is considered one of his best works. Away with such books! Keep them away from Christians. No one can accuse me of overstating the case, or of condemning what I do not understand. Dear friend, I know what I am talking about. I know my Aristotle as well as you or the likes of you. I have lectured on him and have been lectured at on him,[129] and I understand him better than St. Thomas or Duns Scotus did.[130] I can boast about this without arrogance, and if necessary, I can prove it. It makes no difference to me that so many great minds have devoted their labor to him for so many centuries.

Scottish philosopher and theologian Duns Scotus (c. 1266–1308), also known as Doctor Subtilis (the subtle doctor). Painting by Justus Van Ghent (1410–1480).

129. During his first year in Wittenberg (1508–1509), Luther gave lectures on Aristotle's *Nichomachean Ethics*. He had been required to study Aristotle during his student years. See above, pp. 76–78.

130. Duns Scotus (c. 1266–1308), as thoroughgoing an Aristotelian as Thomas Aquinas, was the latter's chief rival for first place among medieval theologians.

Such objections do not disturb me as once they did, for it is plain as day that other errors have remained for even more centuries in the world and in the universities.

I would gladly agree to keeping Aristotle's books *Logic, Rhetoric,* and *Poetics,* or at least keeping and using them in an abridged form, as useful in training young people to speak and to preach properly. But the commentaries and notes must be abolished,[131] and as Cicero's *Rhetoric* is read without commentaries and notes, so Aristotle's *Logic* should be read as it is without all these commentaries. But today nobody learns how to speak or how to preach from it. The whole thing has become nothing but a matter for wearying disputation.

In addition to all this, there are, of course, the Latin, Greek, and Hebrew languages, as well as the mathematical disciplines and history.[132] But all this I commend to the experts. In fact, reform would come readily if only we devoted ourselves seriously to it. Actually a great deal depends on it, for it is here in the universities that the Christian youth and our nobility, with whom the future of Christendom lies, will be educated and trained. Therefore, I believe that there is no work more worthy of pope or emperor than a thorough reform of the universities. And on the other hand, nothing could be more devilish or disastrous than unreformed universities.

I leave it to the physicians to reform their own faculties; I take the jurists and theologians for myself.[133] I say first that it would be a good thing if canon law were completely blotted out, from the first letter to the last, especially the Decretals.*t* More than enough is written in the Bible about how we should behave in all circumstances. The study of canon law only hinders the study of the Holy Scriptures. Moreover, the greater part smacks of nothing but greed and pride. Even if there were much in it that was good, it should still be destroyed, for the pope has the whole canon law imprisoned in the chamber of his heart,[134] so that hence-

131. I.e., the commentaries by the Scholastics. By this time, the curriculum at Wittenberg had all but discarded medieval commentators in rhetoric and logic in favor of Philipp Melanchthon's humanist work (published in 1519 and 1521 [on rhetoric] and 1520 [on logic]).

132. These subjects, with the exception of history, were part of the curriculum in Wittenberg since 1518.

133. In addition to the basic arts faculty, discussed in the previous paragraph, there were three higher faculties at all medieval universities: medicine, law, and theology.

134. German: *in seynis hertzen kasten,* which is Luther's rendering of the Latin *in scrinio pectoris* (further on in

t   I.e., the *Liber Decretalium Gregorii IX* (1234); see p. 383, n. 15. It was an important subject in the faculty of theology.

forth any study of it is just a waste of time and a farce. These days canon law is not what is written in the books of law, but whatever the pope and his flatterers want. Your cause may be thoroughly established in canon law, but the pope always has his "chamber of the heart" in the matter, and all law, and with it the whole world, has to be guided by that. Now it is often a villain, and even the devil himself who controls the chamber, and they proudly boast that it is the Holy Spirit who controls it! Thus they deal with Christ's poor people. They impose many laws upon them but obey none themselves. They compel others to obey these laws or buy their way out with money.

Since then the pope and his followers have suspended the whole canon law as far as they themselves are concerned, and since they pay it no heed but give thought only to their own wanton will, we should do as they do and discard these volumes. Why should we waste our time studying them? We could never fathom the arbitrary will of the pope, which is all that canon law has become. Let canon law perish in God's name, for it arose in the devil's name. Let there be no more "doctors of the Decretals" in the world, but only "doctors of the papal chamber [of his heart]" that is, the pope's flatterers. It is said that there is no better secular government anywhere than among the Turks,[135] who have neither canon law nor secular law but only their Koran. But we must admit that there is no more shameful rule than ours with its canon and secular law, which has resulted in nobody living according to common sense, much less according to Holy Scripture anymore.

Secular law—God help us—has become a wilderness.[136] Though it is much better, wiser, and more honest than the spiritual law,*u* which has nothing good about it except its name, there is nevertheless far too much of it. Surely, wise rulers, along with Holy Scripture, would be more than enough law. As St. Paul says in 1 Cor. 6[:5-6], "Is there no one among you who can judge his neighbor's cause, that you must go to law before heathen courts?" It seems just

u I.e., canon law.

this paragraph and in the one that follows, he uses the Latin phrase), traditionally translated into English as "shrine of the heart." A *scrinium* was a chest or box for the storage of books and papers and, later, relics. According to Pope Boniface VIII, the pope had all laws in his *scrinium pectoris* (literally, "in the storage box of his heart") and was the final judge of its meaning and application. See Friedberg 2:937; LW 31:385 (*Why the Books of the Pope and His Disciples Were Burned*, 1520); and *Smalcald Articles*, III.8.4, in BC, 322.

135. See p. 394, n. 32.

136. By "secular law" Luther means primarily Roman law as codified in the *Corpus Iuris Civilis*, which, together with the *Corpus Iuris Canonici*, constituted the "common law" (*ius commune*) of the Holy Roman Empire (i.e., the law that applied to all cases not governed by a recognized local law, custom, or privilege). In addition, there were various versions of Germanic law that were in the process of being replaced by Roman law or integrated into it, to the advantage of centralizing governments and the disadvantage of local customs and privileges. See Gerald Strauss, *Law, Resistance, and the State: The Opposition to Roman Law in Reformation Germany* (Princeton: Princeton University Press, 1986), ch. 3.

137. By 1530 Luther would have arrived at a far more positive attitude toward Roman law, deeming it the epitome of God-given wisdom in the secular realm, and a correspondingly harsher attitude toward Germanic law, which he found barbarous in its severity and frequently unfair in its application. See James Estes, "Luther's Attitude toward the Legal Traditions of His Time," *Luther-Jahrbuch* 76 (2009): 87–88, 96–99.

138. That is, on the *Four Books of Sentences* (*Sententiarum libri quatuor*) in which the twelfth-century theologian Peter Lombard (c. 1096–1164), who was known as "the Master of the *Sentences*," collected and briefly explained the opinions (*sententiae*) of ancient church fathers on a wide range of theological subjects. As part of their progress toward doctorates, theologians (including Luther) had to lecture on the *Sentences*, which in Luther's day was still the basic textbook for theological instruction.

139. The first degree granted to a candidate in theology was that of bachelor of the Bible (*baccalaureus biblicus*), which qualified the recipient to lecture on the Bible. The next

to me that territorial laws and customs should take precedence over general imperial laws, and that the imperial laws be used only in case of necessity. Would God that every land were ruled by its own brief laws suitable to its gifts and peculiar character. This is how these lands were ruled before these imperial laws were designed, and as many lands are still ruled without them! Rambling and farfetched laws are only a burden to the people, and they hinder cases more than they help them. But I hope that others have already given more thought and attention to this matter than I am able to do.[137]

My dear theologians have saved themselves worry and work. They just leave the Bible alone and lecture on the *Sentences*.[138] I should have thought that the *Sentences* ought to be the first study for young students of theology, and the Bible left to the doctors. But today it is the other way round. The Bible comes first and is then put aside when the baccalaureate is received. The *Sentences* come last, and they occupy a doctor as long as he lives.[139] There is such a solemn obligation attached to these *Sentences* that a person who is not a priest may well lecture on the Bible, but the sentences must be lectured on by someone who is a priest. As I see it, a married man may well be a Doctor of the Bible, but under no circumstances could he be a Doctor of the *Sentences*.[140] How can we prosper when we behave so wrongly and give the Bible, the holy word of God, a back seat? To make things worse, the pope commands in the strongest language that his words are to be studied in the schools and used in the courts, but very little is thought of the gospel. Consequently, the gospel lies neglected in the schools and in the courts. It is pushed aside under the bench and gathers dust so that the scandalous laws of the pope alone may have full sway.

If we bear the name and title of teachers of Holy Scripture, then by this criterion we ought to be compelled to teach the Holy Scripture and nothing else, although we all know that this high and mighty title is much too exalted for a person to take pride in it and allow being designated a Doctor of Holy Scripture. Yet that title might be permitted if the work justified the name. But nowadays, the *Sentences* alone dominate in such a way that we find among the theologians more pagan and human darkness than holy and certain doctrine of Scripture. What are we to do about it? I know of nothing else to do than to pray humbly to God to give us such real doctors of theology as we have in mind. Pope, emperor, and universities may make doctors of arts, of medicine, of laws, of the *Sentences*; but be assured that no one can make a doctor of Holy Scripture except the Holy Spirit from heaven. As Christ says in John 6[:45], "They must all be taught by God himself." Now the Holy Spirit does not care about red or brown birettas[141] or other decorations. Nor does he ask whether a person is young or old, lay or cleric, monk or secular, unmarried or married. In fact, in ancient times he actually spoke through a donkey against the prophet who was riding it [Num. 22:28]. Would God that we were worthy to have such doctors given to us, regardless of whether they were lay or cleric, married or single! They now try to force the Holy Spirit into pope, bishops, and doctors, although there is not the slightest sign or indication whatever that he is in them.

The number of books on theology must be reduced and only the best ones published. It is not many books that make people learned or even much reading. It is, rather, a good book frequently read, no matter how small it is, that makes a person learned in the Scriptures and upright. Indeed, the writings of all the holy Fathers should be read only for a time so that through them we may be led into the Scriptures. As it is, however, we only read them these days to avoid going any further and getting into the Bible. We are like people who read the signposts and never travel the road they indicate. Our dear Fathers wanted to lead us to the Scriptures by their writings, but we use their works to get away from the Scriptures. Nevertheless, the Scripture alone is our vineyard in which we must all labor and toil.[142]

Above all, the foremost reading for everybody, both in the universities and in the schools, should be Holy Scripture—and for the younger boys, the Gospels. And would God that every town had a girls' school as well, where the girls would be taught the gospel for an hour every day either in German

degree was that of bachelor of the sentences (*baccalaureus sententiarius*), which obligated the recipient to lecture on Lombard's *Sentences*. After mastering the first two of the four books of the *Sentences*, the candidate became a *baccalaureus sententiarius formatus* or licentiate, which obliged him to participate in disputations and other academic functions. Then came the doctorate. For Luther's (unusually rapid) traversal of these stages of promotion, see Brecht 1:125–27.

140. At Wittenberg, this pattern was reversed in the case of Philip Melanchthon, who received his bachelor of Bible in 1519 under Luther's direction but never lectured on the *Sentences*. Instead, he was married (in 1520) and developed a new kind of lecture on main topics of Christian doctrine, derived especially from Paul's letter to the Romans, which were published in 1521 as the *Loci communes theologici* ("Theological Common Places").

141. A red biretta was the headdress of a doctor of theology; a brown or russett (*braunrot*) one was that of a master in the arts faculty.

142. Cf. the much later painting by Lucas Cranach Jr. (1515–1586), in the Wittenberg City Church, "The Vineyard of the Lord," which depicted the reformers as vinedressers.

or in Latin.[v] But real schools! Monasteries and nunneries began long ago with that end in view,[w] and it was a praiseworthy and Christian purpose, as we learn from the story of St. Agnes and of other saints.[x] Those were the days of holy virgins and martyrs when all was well with Christendom. But today these monasteries and nunneries have come to nothing but praying and singing. Is it not only right that every Christian know the entire holy gospel by the age of nine or ten? Does not each person derive name and life from the gospel? A spinner or a seamstress teaches her daughter her craft in her early years. But today even the great, learned prelates and the very bishops do not know the gospel.

Oh, how irresponsibly we deal with these poor young people who are committed to us for training and instruction. We shall have to render a solemn account of our neglect to set the word of God before them. Their lot is as described by Jeremiah in Lam. 2[:11-12], "My eyes are grown weary with weeping, my bowels are terrified, my heart is poured out upon the ground because of the destruction of the daughter of my people, for the youth and the children perish in all the streets of the entire city. They said to their mothers, 'Where is bread and wine?' as they fainted like wounded men in the streets of the city and gave up the ghost on their mothers' bosom." We do not see this pitiful evil, how today the young people of Christendom languish and perish miserably in our midst for want of the gospel, in which we ought to be giving them constant instruction and training.

Moreover, even if the universities were diligent in [the teaching of] Holy Scripture, we should not send everybody there as we do now, where their only concern is numbers and where everybody wants a doctor's degree. We should send only the most highly qualified students who have been well trained in the lower schools. Every prince or city coun-

---

v   On this, including the need of schools for girls, see Luther's *To the Councilmen of All Cities in Germany, That They Establish and Maintain Christian Schools* (1524), LW 45:339–78.

w   See p. 423, n. 87.

x   See p. 423, n. 88.

cil should see to this, and permit only the well qualified to be sent. I would advise no one to send his child where the Holy Scriptures are not supreme. Everything that does not unceasingly pursue the study of God's word must corrupt, and because of this we can see what kind of people there are and will be in the universities. Nobody is to blame for this except the pope, the bishops, and the prelates, for it is they who are charged with the welfare of young people. The universities only ought to turn out people who are experts in the Holy Scriptures, who can become bishops and priests, and can stand in the front line against heretics, the devil, and the whole world. But where do you find that? I greatly fear that the universities, unless they teach the Holy Scriptures diligently and impress them on the young students, are wide gates of hell.

26.[y] I know full well that the gang in Rome will allege and trumpet mightily that the pope took the Holy Roman Empire from the Greek emperor and bestowed it upon the Germans, for which honor and benevolence he is said to have justly deserved and obtained submission, thanks, and all good things from the Germans.[143] For this reason they will, perhaps, undertake to throw all attempts to reform themselves to the four winds and will not allow us to think about anything but the bestowal of the Roman Empire. For this cause they have persecuted and oppressed many a worthy emperor so willfully and arrogantly that it is a shame even to mention it.[z] And with the same adroitness they have made themselves overlords of every secular power and authority, contrary to the holy gospel. I must therefore speak of this, too.

There is no doubt that the true Roman Empire, which the writings of the prophets foretold in Num. 24[:17-24] and Dan. 2[:36-45], has long since been overthrown and come

143. Through a series of military conquests, Charles the Great (a.k.a. Charlemagne, c. 742–814), king of the Franks, managed to unite most of western Europe under one rule for the first time since the collapse of the western Roman Empire in the fifth century. In the year 800 Charles had himself crowned "Emperor of the Romans" by Pope Leo III (750–816) in St. Peter's Basilica, an act that nullified any claim by the Byzantine emperors in Constantinople to authority in what had been the western Empire. Thereafter Charlemagne and his successors as German kings were known as Roman emperors. In later struggles with the German emperors over who possessed the highest jurisdiction, medieval popes interpreted Charlemagne's coronation by Leo as the act of someone who, by virtue of his supreme jurisdiction in both secular and spiritual matters, had the authority to take imperial power from the Greek emperor and bestow it on the Frankish king. The pope's confirmation was deemed necessary for the election of the German king/Roman emperor to be deemed valid, and that confirmation could be withheld or withdrawn.

y   This entire section is missing from the first printing of the treatise; Luther added it to the second printing; see p. 418, note *n*.

z   See p. 379, n. 9.

144. Luther here dissociates himself in part from the conception of "world history" that had prevailed in western Europe in the Middle Ages. It was based on the prophecy in Daniel 2 (repeated in variant form in Daniel 7) of the rise and fall of the four great empires of "gold," "silver," "bronze," and "iron" (with the latter to be divided into empires of "iron" and "clay") that would precede the apocalypse and the establishment of Christ's kingdom. Medieval exegetes identified the four empires as Babylon, Persia, Greece (Macedonia), and Rome. For as long as the apocalypse had not occurred, it remained necessary to argue that the Roman Empire still existed. Hence, theologians argued that the collapse of the western Roman Empire in 476 left imperial authority intact in the eastern Empire (Byzantium) and that the papal coronation of Charlemagne in 800 effected a transfer of imperial rule from the Greeks to the Germans (*translatio imperii a Graecis ad Germanos*). See above, n. 143.

to an end,[144] as Balaam clearly prophesied in Num. 24[:24] when he said, "The Romans shall come and overthrow the Jews, and afterward they also shall be destroyed."[145] That happened under the Goths,[146] but more particularly when the empire of the Turks began almost a thousand years ago. Then eventually Asia and Africa fell away, and in time France and Spain, and finally Venice broke away, and nothing was left to Rome of its former power.

When, then, the pope could not subdue to his arrogant will the Greeks and the emperor at Constantinople, who was the hereditary Roman emperor, he invented a little device to rob this emperor of his empire and his title and to turn it over to the Germans, who at that time were warlike and of good repute. In so doing, [the Romanists] brought the power of the Roman Empire under their control so that it had to be held as a fief from them. And this is just what happened. [Imperial authority] was taken away from the emperor at Constantinople, and its name and title given to us Germans, and thereby we became servants of the pope. There is now a second Roman Empire, built by the pope upon the Germans, for the former one, as I said earlier, has long since fallen.

So, then, the Roman See now gets its own way. It has taken possession of Rome, driven out the German emperor, and bound him by oaths not to dwell at Rome.[a] He is supposed to be Roman emperor, and yet he is not to have possession of Rome; and besides, he is to be dependent on and move within the limits of the good pleasure of the pope and his supporters. We have the title, but they have the land and the city. They have always abused our simplicity to serve their own arrogant and tyrannical designs. They call us crazy Germans for letting them make fools and monkeys of us as they please.

Now then, it is a small thing for God to toss empires and principalities to and fro. He is so gentle with them that once in a while he gives a kingdom to a scoundrel and takes one from a good man, sometimes by the treachery of wicked,

a   According to the *Donation of Constantine* (cf. n. 110); see Mirbt-Aland, 255, no. 504, §§17–19.

faithless men, and sometimes by inheritance. This is what we read about the kingdoms of Persia and Greece, and about almost all kingdoms. It says in Dan. 2[:21] and 4[:34-35], "He who rules over all things dwells in heaven, and it is he alone who overthrows kingdoms, tosses them to and fro, and establishes them." Since no one, particularly a Christian, can think it a very great thing to receive a kingdom, we Germans, too, need not lose our heads because a new Roman Empire is bestowed on us. For in God's eyes it is but a trifling gift, one that he often gives to the most unworthy, as it says in Dan. 4[:35], "All who dwell on earth are as nothing in his eyes, and he has the power in all the kingdoms of men to give them to whom he will."

But although the pope used violence and unjust means to rob the true emperor of his Roman Empire, or of the title of his Roman Empire, and gave it to us Germans, yet it is nevertheless certain that God has used the pope's wickedness to give such an empire to the German nation, and after the fall of the first Roman Empire, to set up another, the one that now exists. And although we had nothing to do with this wickedness of the popes, and although we did not understand their false aims and purposes, we have nevertheless paid tragically and far too dearly for such an empire with incalculable bloodshed, with the suppression of our liberty, the occupation and theft of all our possessions, especially of our churches and benefices, and with the suffering of unspeakable deception and insult. We carry the title of empire, but it is the pope who has our wealth, honor, body, life, soul, and all that we possess. This is how they deceive the Germans and cheat them with tricks.[b] What the popes have sought was to be emperors themselves, and though they could not achieve this, they nonetheless succeeded in setting themselves over the emperors.

Since the Empire has been given us by the providence of God as well as by the plotting of evil men, without any guilt

---

145. NRSV: "But ships shall come from Kittim and shall afflict Asshur and Eber." Luther follows the Vulgate, which translates "They will come in ships from Italy and be over the Assyrians and destroy the Hebrews," In the 1523 translation into German, Luther leaves the Hebrew Kittim in the text and in a marginal note insists that it applies rather to Macedonia (Greece) and Alexander the Great (356-323 BCE). In his lectures on Genesis from 1537, Luther associates Kittim primarily with Greece but also with the coasts of Italy and France (LW 2:191). In the 1545 edition of the German Bible, he explains that Kittim refers to both Alexander the Great and the Romans, whose kingdoms will collapse, leaving only Israel (WA DB 8:514-15).

146. The Visigoths sacked Rome in the year 410.

---

b   *Szo sol man die Deutschen teuschen und mit teuschen teuschen*, a pun on *Deutchen* ("Germans"), *teuschen* ("deceive," "cheat"), and *teuschen* ("tricks," "deceptions") that cannot be duplicated in English.

on our part, I shall not advise that we give it up, but rather that we rule it wisely and in the fear of God, as long as it pleases him for us to rule it. For, as has been said already, it does not matter to him where an empire comes from; his will is that it be governed regardless. Though the popes were dishonest in taking it from others, we were not dishonest in receiving it. It has been given us through evil people by the will of God, for which we have more regard that for the fraudulent intention to be emperors themselves, and indeed more than emperors, and only to mock and ridicule us with the title. The king of Babylon also seized his kingdom by robbery and violence. Yet it was God's will that that kingdom be ruled by the holy princes Daniel, Hananiah, Azariah, and Mishael.[c] Much more, then, is it God's will that this empire should be ruled by the Christian princes of Germany, no matter whether the pope stole it, got it by force, or established it anew. It is all God's ordering, which came to pass before we knew about it.

Therefore, the pope and his followers have no right to boast that they have done the German nation a great favor by giving us the Roman Empire. In the first place, they did not mean it for our good. Rather, they took advantage of our simplicity when they did it in order to strengthen their proud designs against the real Roman emperor at Constantinople, from whom the pope took his empire against God and right, which he had no authority to do. In the second place, the pope's intention was not to give us the Empire, but to get it for himself, so that he might bring all our power, our freedom, our wealth, our souls, and our bodies into subjection to himself, and through us (had God not prevented it) to subdue all the world. He clearly says so himself in his Decretals,[d] and has attempted to do so by means of many wicked wiles with a number of the German emperors. Thus have we Germans been beautifully neatly taught our

---

c   Dan. 1:6-7; 2:48; 5:29. The latter three are renamed in Dan. 1:7— Shadrach, Meshach, and Abednego.

d   See, e.g., the decretal *Venerabilem fratrem* (1202). See Mirbt-Aland 307, no. 596; Friedberg 2:80.

German.[e] While we supposed we were going to be lords, we became in fact servants of the most deceitful tyrants of all time. We have the name, the title, and the insignia of empire, but the pope has its treasures, authority, rights, and liberties. The pope gobbles the kernel while we are left playing with the husk.

Now may God, who (as I said) tossed this empire into our lap by the wiles of tyrants and has charged us with its rule, help us to live up to the name, title, and insignia and to retrieve our liberty. Let the Romanists see once and for all what it is that we have received from God through them. If they boast that they have bestowed an empire on us, let them. If that is true, then let the pope give us back Rome and all that he has gotten from the Empire; let him free our land from his intolerable taxing and fleecing; let him give us back our liberty, our rights, our honor, our body and soul; and let the Empire be what an empire should be, so that the pope's words and pretensions might be fulfilled.

If he will not do that, then what is he playing at with his false, fabricated words and his deceptions? Has there not for so many centuries now been enough of his ceaseless and uncouth leading of this noble nation around by the nose? It does not follow that the pope must be above the emperor because he crowns or appoints him. The prophet St. Samuel anointed and crowned the kings Saul and David at God's command, and yet he was their subject.[f] The prophet Nathan anointed King Solomon,[g] but he was not set over the king on that account. Similarly, St. Elisha had one of his servants anoint Jehu king of Israel, but they still remained obedient and subject to the king.[h] It has never happened in all the history of the world that he who consecrated or crowned the king was over the king, except in this single instance of the pope.

e   Probably a pun similar to note *b*, p. 457, meaning "We Germans have been tricked [by the popes]."

f   1 Sam. 10:1; 16:13.

g   1 Kgs. 1:39. It was in fact Zadok the priest who anointed Solomon.

h   2 Kgs. 9:6.

The pope permits himself to be crowned by three cardinals who are beneath him, but he is nonetheless their superior. Why should he then go against his own example, against universal practice, and against the teaching of Scripture by exalting himself above secular authority or imperial majesty simply because he crowns or consecrates the emperor? It is quite enough that he is the emperor's superior in the things of God, that is, in preaching, teaching, and the administration of the sacraments. In these respects, any bishop and any priest is over everybody else, just as St. Ambrose in his diocese was over the emperor Theodosius,[147] the prophet Nathan over David, and Samuel over Saul. Therefore, let the German emperor be really and truly emperor. Let neither his authority nor his power be suppressed by such sham pretensions of these papist deceivers as though they were to be excepted from his authority and were themselves to rule in all things.

27.[i] Enough has now been said about the failings of the clergy, though you may and will find more if you look in the right place. Let us now take a look at some of those of the secular realm.

In the first place, there is a great need for a general law and decree in the German nation against boundlessly excessive and costly dress, because of which so many nobles and rich people are impoverished.[j] God has certainly given us, as he has to other countries, enough wool, flax, linen, and everything else necessary for the seemly and honorable dress of every class. We do not need to waste fantastic sums for silk, velvet, golden ornaments, and foreign wares. I believe that even if the pope had not robbed us with his intolerable fleecing, we would still have more than enough of these home-grown robbers, the traders in silk and velvet. We see that now everybody wants to be like everybody else, and pride and envy are thereby aroused and increased among us, as we deserve. All this misery and much more besides would

147. In the year 390, St. Ambrose, bishop of Milan, refused to admit Emperor Theodosius I (347–395) to communion until after he had done public penance for having ordered the indiscriminate slaughter of seven thousand inhabitants of Thessalonica following the murder there of the Roman governor by rioters.

---

i   In the first printing of the treatise, this section followed immediately after section 25 and was numbered 26.

j   Such a law (part of a larger *Polizeiordunung*) was proposed at the Diet of Worms in 1521; see RTA 2:335–41.

probably be avoided if only our ardor [for such things] would let us be thankfully content with the good things God has already given us.

It is also necessary to restrict the traffic in spices, which is another of the great ships in which money is carried out of the German lands. By the grace of God, more things to eat and drink grow here than in any other country, and they are just as tasty and good. Perhaps my proposals seem foolish, impractical, and give the impression that I want to ruin the greatest of all trades, that of commerce. But I am doing my best, and if there is no general improvement in these matters, then let him who will try his hand at improving them. I do not see that many good morals have ever come to a country through commerce, and in ancient times God made his people Israel dwell away from the sea because of this and did not let them engage in much commerce.[k]

But the greatest misfortune of the German nation is certainly the *zynskauf*.[148] If that did not exist, many people[l] would have to leave unpurchased their silks, velvets, golden ornaments, spices, and display of every kind. This traffic has not existed much longer than a hundred years, and it has already brought almost all princes, endowed institutions, cities, nobles, and their heirs to poverty, misery, and ruin. If it goes on for another hundred years, Germany will not have a penny left, and the chances are we shall have to eat one another. The devil invented the practice, and by confirming it the pope has brought woe upon the whole world.

Therefore, I beg and pray at this point that everyone open their eyes and see the ruin of their children and heirs. Ruin is not just at the door, it is already in the house. I pray and beseech emperor, princes, lords, and city councilors to condemn this trade as speedily as possible and prevent it from now on, regardless of whether the pope with all his unjust justice objects, or whether benefices or monasteries are based upon it. It is better for a city to have one benefice supported by honest legacies or revenue than to have a hundred

148. *Zinskauf* in modern German, a synonym for *Rentenkauf*, i.e., the purchase of an annuity (a yearly rent) in return for the use of a sum of money or a piece of property. Because the buyer was theoretically purchasing something and could not recall the sum paid, the annual payments could not be called interest. In this way the biblical and canon-law prohibitions of lending at interest to other Christians (usury) was circumvented. Luther, who was more conservative on the subject of charging interest than were his Catholic opponents, like Johann Eck, insisted that the *Zinskauf* was indeed usurious unless rigorous standards of fairness (e.g., equal risk on the part of both buyer and seller) were met. See his *Treatise on Good Works* (p. 346, n. 118), and his *Long Sermon on Usury* (early 1520); LW 45:233–43 (helpful introduction), 273–95 (text); and Brecht 1:356–57.

---

k   See Ezek. 27:3, 8; and Isa. 23:1, 8, where Tyre is described, in contrast to Israel, as having merchant ships and being engaged in commerce.

l   Singular in the original.

benefices supported by *zynskauf.* Indeed, a benefice supported by a *zynskauf* is more grievous and oppressive than twenty supported by legacies. In fact, the *zynskauf* must be a sign and proof that the world has been sold to the devil because of its grievous sins and that at the same time we are losing both temporal and spiritual possessions. And yet we do not even notice it.

In this connection, we must put a bit in the mouth of the Fuggers and similar companies.*ᵐ* How is it possible in the lifetime of one person to accumulate such great possessions, worthy of a king, legally and according to God's will? I don't know. But what I really cannot understand is how a person with one hundred gulden can make a profit of twenty in one year. Nor, for that matter, can I understand how a person with one gulden can make another—and make it not from tilling the soil or raising cattle, where the increase of wealth depends not on human wit but on God's blessing. I leave this to people who understand the ways of the world.[149] As a theologian I have no further reproof to make on this subject except that it has an evil and offending appearance, about which St. Paul says, "Avoid every appearance or show of evil" [1 Thess. 5:22]. I know full well that it would be a far godlier thing to increase agriculture and decrease commerce. I also know that those who work on the land and seek their livelihood from it according to the Scriptures do far better. All this was said to us and to everybody else in the story of Adam, "Cursed be the ground when you work it; it shall bear you thistles and thorns, and in the sweat of your face you shall eat your bread" [Gen. 3:17-19]. There is still a lot of land lying fallow and neglected.

Next comes the abuse of eating and drinking, which gives us Germans a bad reputation in foreign lands, as though it were a special vice of ours. Preaching cannot stop it so deeply is it rooted and so firmly has it got the upper hand. The waste of money would be insignificant were it not for all the vices that accompany it—murder, adultery, stealing, blasphemy, and every other form of immorality. Govern-

149. Luther here reflects the Aristotelian economic principle that money is simply an object like a chair or table and thus incapable of making money.

m See p. 406, n. 57.

ment can do something to prevent it; otherwise, what Christ says will come to pass, that the last day shall come like a secret snare, when they shall be eating and drinking, marrying and wooing, building and planting, buying and selling." It is so much like what is now going on that I sincerely hope the Judgment Day is at hand, although very few people give it any thought.

Finally, is it not lamentable that we Christians tolerate open and common brothels in our midst, when all of us are baptized unto chastity?° I know perfectly well what some say to this, that is, that it is not a custom peculiar to one nation, that it would be difficult to put a stop to it, and, moreover, that it is better to keep such a house than that married women, or girls, or others of still more honorable estate should be molested. Nevertheless, should not secular and Christian governments consider that one ought not to counteract these things in such a heathen manner? If the children of Israel could exist without such impropriety, why cannot Christians do as much? In fact, how do so many cities, country towns, market towns, and villages do without such houses? Why can't large cities do without them as well?

In this matter and in the other matters previously mentioned, I have tried to point out how many good works secular government could do, and what the duty of every government should be, so that everyone may learn what an awful responsibility it is to rule and sit in high places. What use would it be if a ruler were himself as holy as St. Peter, if he did not diligently try to help his subjects in these matters? His very authority would condemn him. It is the duty of governing authority to seek the best for its subjects. But if the authorities were to give some thought to how young people might be brought together in marriage, the hope of married life would greatly help every one of them to endure and resist temptation.

But today everybody is attracted to the priesthood or the monastic life, and among them, I am sorry to say, there is

---

n   Cf. Luke 21:34; 12:45, and Matt. 24:36-44.
o   See above, *Treatise on Good Works*, p. 347.

not one in a hundred who has any other reason than that he seeks a living and doubts that he will ever be able to support himself in married life. Therefore, they live wildly enough beforehand, and wish, as they say, to get it out of their system, but experience shows that it is only more deeply embedded in them. I find the proverb true, "Despair makes most monks and priests."[p] That is what happens and that is how it is, as we see.

I will, however, sincerely advise that to avoid the many sins that spread so shamelessly, neither youths nor maidens should bind themselves to chastity or clerical life before the age of thirty. Chastity, as St. Paul says, is a special gift [1 Cor. 7:7]. Therefore, I would advise those upon whom God has not conferred his special gift to abstain from clerical life and making vows. I say further that if you trust God so little that you fear you won't be able to support yourself as a married man, and you wish to become a cleric only because of this distrust, then I beg you for your own soul's sake not to become a cleric at all, but rather a farmer or anything you like. For where a single measure of faith in God is needed to earn your daily bread, there must be ten times that amount of faith to remain a cleric. If you do not trust God to provide for you in temporal things, how will you trust him to support you in spiritual things? Alas, unbelief and distrust spoil everything and lead us into all kinds of misery, as we see in all walks of life.

Much more could be said of this pitiful state of affairs. Young people have nobody to watch over them. They all do as they please, and the government is as much use to them as if it did not exist. And yet the care of young people ought to be the chief concern of the pope, bishops, rulers, and councils. They want to exercise authority far and wide, and yet they help nobody. For just this reason a lord and ruler will be a rare sight in heaven, even though he build a hundred churches for God and raise up all the dead!

Let this suffice for the moment. [I think I have said enough in my little book *Treatise on Good Works*[q] about what

---

p   Wander, 4:1625.

the secular authorities and the nobility ought to do. There is certainly room for improvement in their lives and in their rule, yet the abuses of the temporal power are not to be compared with those of the spiritual power, as I have shown in that book.]ʳ

I know full well that I have sung rather grandly. I have made many suggestions that will be considered impractical. I have attacked many things too severely. But how else ought I to do it? I am duty-bound to speak. These are the things I would do if I were able. I would rather have the wrath of the world upon me than the wrath of God. The world can do no more to me than take my life. In the past I have made frequent overtures of peace to my enemies, but as I see, God has compelled me through them to open my mouth ever wider and to give them enough to say, bellow, shout, and write because they have nothing else to do. Well, I know another little song about Rome and the Romanists. If their ears are itching to hear it, I will sing that one to them, too—and pitch it in the highest key! You understand what I mean, dear Rome.[150]

Moreover, I have many times offered my writings for investigation and hearing, but to no avail because, as I too know full well, if my cause is just, it must be condemned on earth and be justified by Christ alone in heaven. For all the Scriptures bear witness that the cause of Christians and of Christendom must be judged by God alone, and no cause has ever yet been justified on earth by human effort because the opposition has always been too great and too strong. It is still my greatest concern and anxiety that my cause may not be condemned, by which I would know for certain that it is not yet pleasing to God. Therefore, just let them go hard at it, pope, bishop, priest, monk, or scholar. They are just the ones to persecute the truth, as they have always done. May God give us all a Christian mind and grant to the Christian nobility of the German nation in particular true spiritual courage to do the best they can for the poor church. Amen.

Wittenberg, in the year 1520.

150. The "little song" is *The Babylonian Captivity of the Church* (LW 36:3–126), which was also written in 1520, shortly after this treatise was published.

q   See above, pp. 342–47.

r   The bracketed passage was inserted into the second edition of the treatise. See above, p. 418f., note *n*..

Image Credits